Mark St.

The politics of a Tudor merchant adventurer

The politics of a Tudor merchant adventurer

A letter to the Earls of East Friesland

edited with an
introduction by
G. D. Ramsay

Manchester University Press

Published by Manchester University Press
Oxford Road, Manchester M13 9PL

British Library cataloguing in publication data

Nedham, George
The politics of a Tudor merchant adventurer.
1. England – Commerce – Netherlands – History
– Sources
2. Netherlands – Commerce – England – History
– Sources
I. Title II. Ramsay, George Daniel
382'.0942'0492 HF3518.N/

ISBN 0-7190-0754-2

Phototypeset in V.I.P. Bembo by
Western Printing Services Ltd, Bristol

Printed in Great Britain by
The Pitman Press, Bath

Contents

Preface

This little book has arisen out of some longstanding investigations into the history of the Company of Merchants Adventurers of England. It is many years since the 'Letter to the Earls of East Friesland', ostensibly by 'W.G.', caught my attention as a source of information. The authorship remained a baffling problem until the essential clue was supplied by a missive, unsigned and undated but written *c.* 1568, the original of which is in the Pepysian Library at Magdalene College, Cambridge. As further evidence accumulated, the lively and original but forgotten personality of George Nedham came to life under my eyes as the indubitable composer of the 'Letter'. In the Introduction, I have attempted to explain why it remains an important historical document, and to summarise what can be discovered about Nedham and why he wrote it.

My gratitude is owed to the owners and custodians of the extant copies of the 'Letter', as also to the various friends and colleagues who have helped me with advice on sundry points. I am particularly obliged to Earl Fitzwilliam, owner of the copy on which I have relied most to establish my text, and to Mr P. I. King, Chief Archivist of the Northamptonshire Record Office, in whose care the precious document reposes. My thanks are also due to Miss Jean Imray, Archivist to the Mercers' Company of London, for facilitating my consultation of the documents in her charge. My son Nigel commented on the typescript of my introduction, and my wife has given invaluable help with the proofs.

G. D. Ramsay

Oxford, 14 May 1979

Introduction

I
A literary tradition

The text here presented sheds some light upon sixteenth-century London and Antwerp. It is also notable as an example of an unusual literary *genre* – a discourse upon contemporary commerce and politics by a merchant. Sixteenth-century merchants as a category were comparatively inarticulate; their particular world is known to us only through the chance survival of some collections of letters and a few account-books, together with the petitions and protests in the public archives. Yet the sixteenth century is by general consent accepted as the age in which the vernacular language at length reached sufficient maturity to provide a means of expression for social and political argument in England, achieving a precedence over the traditional medium of Latin and the neighbouring rival, French. The advance in sheer linguistic capability may be measured by comparing the 'Letter' here printed with its forerunner in the same field *The Libelle of Englyshe Polycye*, dating from little more than a century earlier.[1] A literary tradition, covering economic and political topics, had taken shape. Indeed, the increasing use of the English language for the discussion of public affairs was in its way as remarkable in the sixteenth century as its employment for poems, plays and theological debate, though it must be agreed that wielders of the pen were usually lawyers and clergymen rather than merchants.[2] But whatever the profession of authors of discourses on public affairs, their works have been little regarded by language and literature specialists, who have preferred to focus their interest upon *belles-lettres*, though an honourable exception is provided by one remarkable study of political and social thought, to which the present writer must express his indebtedness.[3]

Certainly the publication of texts concerned with the business of living, as contrasted with literary problems, seems by tacit consent to have devolved upon historians. It is over a century since Reinhold Pauli set the ball rolling by printing the essays of Clement Armstrong on the Staplers and on the restoration of agriculture, to be followed by E. Lamond's edition of *A Discourse of the Common Weal* and R. H. Tawney's of Thomas Wilson's *A Discourse upon Usury* and R. de Roover's of the *Memorandum for the understanding of the Exchange*, to mention only the outstanding items.[4] The list might be prolonged sufficiently to occasion surprise that any significant piece of literature dealing with economic and political affairs in mid sixteenth-century England has hitherto remained unprinted or un-reprinted. George Nedham's 'Letter to the Earls of East Friesland' may, however, be fairly claimed as such. Though nowadays neglected, it is a lively and influential tract of which in its day at least a dozen copies were made, including translations into Latin and German. Though remaining in manuscript, it must have been known to many people. This edition represents an attempt to make it available to the modern reader who already knows something of the sixteenth century in north-western Europe. The text is offered without the embellishment of footnotes, save very occasionally, chiefly to indicate the meaning of a word now obsolete as given in the *Oxford English Dictionary*. It is hoped that in the reasonably full introduction there is embodied sufficient information about the author and his intentions to make unnecessary any elaborate *apparatus criticus*.

The text as set forth in this volume does not purport to be an exact copy of any particular one of the manuscripts, which exhibit the foibles of a variety of copyists.[5] It has been prepared with the intention of rendering a clear but faithful version of the message composed by George Nedham for his readers, with the needs of students of sixteenth-century history specially in mind. Spelling has therefore been modernised, and punctuation and paragraphing supplied. No attempt has otherwise been made to tidy up Nedham's grammar or syntax, though occasionally a (*sic*) has been inserted to disclaim editorial responsibility, and here and there a word has been added in square brackets to assist the reader by clarifying the text. No exception has been made for proper names. Thus Nedham's 'Eastenricke' has been printed as 'Austria' and his 'Duringe' as 'Thuringia', while 'Collomis' has been transliterated as 'Columbus' and 'Fernando' as 'Ferdinand'. Nedham was aware of the problems of nomenclature involved in discussing the political organisation of sixteenth-century Germany, and tended to resolve them summarily. Accordingly, when faced by the need to mention the *Stift* of Utrecht or of Münster, he simply transliterated it into 'stight' – 'gh' being in his time usually pronounced as 'f', as it still is in 'laughter' or 'rough'. 'Stight' is however not an English word. On the other hand, in neither Nedham's day nor our own is there any precise English equivalent for *Stift*, which according to the context may mean 'bishopric', 'see', or 'foundation'. Nedham's 'Stight' has accordingly been replaced in the text by an italic *stift*, without the initial capital.

II
George Nedham

Little is known of the origins of George Nedham, author of 'A Letter to the Earls of East Friesland', save that they were modest though not of the very humblest. It may be surmised that he was born in the mid-1520s. Like many another country youth of his generation, he made his way to London, there to serve as apprentice to a merchant. When he had completed his articles, his name was duly entered in the register of freemen of the City of London on 7 July 1552, when he was described as son of Otwell Nedham, *generosus*, of Snitterton, co. Derby – a hamlet a mile or two to the west of Matlock.[6] Elswhere, there is evidence to indicate that he was the sixth of the seven sons of his father Otwell, so that as a cadet of a small landowning family he can have enjoyed only a meagre material fortune.[7] At London, young George was apprenticed first to Robert Shakerley of the Mercers' Company, with whom he evidently did not stay long. On 10 November 1542, he was exonerated from this first engagement and on 10 July 1543 bound formally to another member of the same Company, Thomas Stacey, whom he served for nine years.[8] This was a term longer than most, but not strikingly exceptional. There is no evidence to indicate that George Nedham had any family connection with the City, though his surname was not unknown among the merchants at this time.[9]

George Nedham's master, Thomas Stacey, like so many members of the Mercers' Company at this time, was active in the trade with Antwerp as a merchant adventurer. But he was no ordinary merchant adventurer, for unlike other members of the fellowship he pursued his commercial interests beyond Antwerp into the continental hinterland, dispatching English wool, presumably acquired at the Calais staple, to Venice.[10] Indeed, it looks as if in the middle of the sixteenth century, in 1544 and later, Stacey was operating from a headquarters at Antwerp rather than London. He was certainly busy at Antwerp in the years 1549–52.[11] He was a merchant of some standing in the City of London, where he served as a warden of the Mercers' Company in 1555–6.[12] It was at Antwerp in 1548 that Nedham, acting as factor for Stacey and another Londoner named John Cosworth, entered into a bargain with a Florentine merchant to barter 104 kerseys for two bales of camlets plus a payment of £54 16*s* Flemish, to be discharged in a month. Nedham was still in the service of Stacey and Cosworth when in 1552 he initiated a lawsuit against one Juan Henriquez, who had made difficulties about paying up his share of the insurance money due for a ship that had been seized by the Scots.[13] These scraps of evidence prove little, but they do suggest that Nedham spent much of his 'prentice years abroad, at the Babylon-like trade metropolis of Antwerp. This helps to explain how he subsequently acquired a Netherlands wife; in fact, she was a well-endowed widow who brought him a house at Bergen-op-Zoom and some landed property near the coast of Holland, yielding him altogether an annual income that he put at £50 sterling.[14]

A close relationship at this time linked the Mercers' Company and the Company of Merchants Adventurers. It was customary when taking up the freedom of one to qualify as a member of the other, and it is to be assumed that Nedham did this. He certainly lost no time in joining the merchants who were shipping woollen cloths from London to Antwerp. The customs roll for 1553–4 indicates that on 16 April 1554 he dispatched forty cloths in his own name, and another couple of dozen followed on 12 July. On 9 August he sent off thirteen 'pieces of worsteds' – an unusual export at this period, though worsteds were manufactured in small quantity in Norfolk.[15] For these consignments he can hardly have laid out less than three hundred pounds in the cloth market at Blackwell Hall, though since trade was buoyant and the market therefore easy it may have been less difficult than usual to raise the money to satisfy the manufacturer.[16] Three years later, he was still in business, when on 3 June 1557 he sent off half-a-dozen cloths, probably to Antwerp.[17] But this was a miserable scale on which to operate. Some of his contemporaries were already organising a turnover of cloths up to a hundred times the size of his.[18] Perhaps he grew discouraged and threw in his hand. In 1561 his former apprentice Jefferey Colinge was duly received into the freedom of the Mercers' Company, and he himself in 1562 was listed among the members 'out of the livery'.[19] It does not appear that he ever achieved the status of a liveryman, nor does his name appear on the customs lists extant for the reign of Elizabeth. It may be that he deserted London for Antwerp, where as a factor for other merchants he might have hoped to earn a better living.

Nedham's experience of life on the continent was by now extensive, stretching far back to his early days as apprentice to Stacey. To judge by his writings, his interest in international politics must have been intense, and he was fuelling it by reading and travel. He moved sufficiently far to make the acquaintance of the young Counts of East Friesland and to observe the harbour facilities at their port of Emden.[20] How far to the south he had penetrated we do not know, but in the service of his master he may well have crossed the Alps and got to Venice. There is no evidence to indicate that he ever travelled further, though it is tempting to wonder if he had a hand in the production of the brief black-letter pamphlet of 1555, *A Warnyng for Englande, conteyning the horrible practises of the King of Spayne, in the Kyngdome of Naples.*[21] The anonymous author was primarily concerned to alert his fellow-countrymen to the horrors in store for them 'if the King of Spain obtain the dominion in England' as a result of the impending marriage of Mary Tudor and the Prince of Spain. The purpose of the sheet was entirely political, but it was evidently written by someone very interested in trade, and it contains lists of the coins current and the taxes payable at Naples. It is to be recalled that at this time the English had virtually ceased to trade through the Straits of Gibraltar into the Mediterranean, and that Nedham's master Stacey was the only merchant adventurer known to traffic across the Alps.[22] A reference to 'the slavery and tyranny used in Naples' in the 1572 postscript to the 'Letter to the Earls of East Friesland' suggests that Nedham at least had an acquaintance with *A Warnyng for Englande.*[23]

But even at Antwerp, there were opportunities for observing the conduct of the universal Habsburg monarchy in some of its less pleasing aspects. In particular, as an English merchant whose livelihood depended upon an uninterrupted flow of traffic between the Scheldt and the Thames, he was alarmed, injured and offended by the periodical interferences of the Netherlands government at Brussels with the movement of Anglo-Netherlands trade. Of this there had been four or five instances, he observed, since Henry VIII in 1544 had captured Boulogne from the French, when the ships of the cloth fleet of the merchants adventurers had been detained until the political situation in England had been ascertained to be satisfactory.[24] The most recent scare had been in 1560, when the English merchants in the middle of their early summer fair were swept by a rumour that the Regent of the Netherlands was about to visit the displeasure of her brother the King of Spain at the English intervention in Scotland by ordering a seizure of their cloths. The Englishmen were panic-stricken, and many of them hastened to sell off their wares at whatever prices they would fetch, without waiting to bargain for a modicum of profit. After two or three days, the alarm subsided, but meanwhile a number of the English merchants had accepted losses. These were recalled in the City as offering yet another example of Habsburg ill-will.[25]

At some relatively early stage in his career, Nedham had been struck by the commercial possibilities of the fishing port and town of Emden, just outside the north-western frontier of the Netherlands. He had drafted a short paper entitled 'Articles of Emden', in which he commended the haven for its accessibility by sea, its excellent communications with the German hinterland, and its convenience for commercial use. Perhaps because England as well as the Netherlands lay under the rule of Philip and Mary, the 'Articles of Emden' were prudently devoid of political matter other than a brief demonstration how the rulers of the East Friesland principality, in which Emden lay, were on good terms with their neighbours in north-western Germany, so that peaceful traders were not likely to meet with any local interference in the conduct of their business.[26] This paper was circulated to an unknown number of people, among whom Nedham liked to think that Elizabeth Tudor, Queen of England since November 1558, was numbered.[27] It seems to have been the market scare of 1560 that led Nedham to recopy these 'Articles of Emden', and prefix to them a highly political disquisition of some five thousand words. Mary Tudor was now dead, England and the Netherlands had developed to separate rulers and the political climate had changed.

The 'Articles of Emden' with their lengthy prologue were cast in the form of a petition or exhortation addressed directly to the new Queen of England from her 'most humble and obedient servant George Nedham'. The whole writing was enshrined in the pages of a thin booklet of some sixteen folios, of which it occupied thirteen: this was 'The Book of George Nedham'.[28] The paper was of fine quality, and the offering was bound within a cover of white vellum stamped with a pattern in gold. In its pristine condition the 'Book' assuredly presented a glittering aspect, as became a volume intended for royal perusal. In his text, Nedham sought to remind the queen how the friendship of her father, brother and sister had in turn been exploited by the Emperor Charles V and his son Philip II for their selfish political designs on the continent, one result of which had been for the English the loss of Calais.[29] As Nedham interpreted the situation, the extraordinary political rise of the Habsburg princes – 'the House of Burgundy', as he called them – had been achieved as a result of the rapid economic development of the Netherlands, 'a base and barren country' which had 'become most wealthy and fruitful' by reason of 'the traffic and access' of the English merchants with their incomparable cloths.[30] The English merchants had thus enabled the House of Burgundy to draw enormous sums of money in taxes from its subjects in the Netherlands, and so increase its political weight; and they were foolishly content, in pursuit of their private profit, every time they fitted out a cloth fleet, blindly to put three or four score ships with their crews, two or three hundred merchants, and commodities worth three or four hundred thousand pounds 'or better' at the mercy of the rulers of Antwerp and the Netherlands.[31]

The situation, as Nedham now saw it, might very simply be remedied by removing the English cloth mart, or part of it, from Antwerp to the town of Emden, so conveniently beyond the frontiers of the Netherlands. In five years, he averred, Emden 'would be made a packhouse for all Europe as Antwerp now is'.[32] Since the queen of England was still the close ally of the king of Spain who was also ruler of the Netherlands, it was a bold action on the part of Nedham to put forward such a proposal. However, he was not advocating any loosening of the alliance, much less any overt political breach. The matter was one simply of spreading risks, he protested, of detaching 'one parcel of your woollen commodity' for sale at Emden and so ensuring a trade foothold outside the Netherlands.[33] Trading might quietly continue at both the Emden and Antwerp market-places, to the great advantage of the queen of England: 'Your Majesty thus having two strings to your bow may so use them as either of them [*sc.* the respective ruling princes] will seek the best they can to please you.'[34] 'The Book of George Nedham' carries some interest as a forerunner to the 'Letter' printed in this volume. Not only are they consistent in politics and general outlook, but there is a good deal of overlapping of statement. The 'Book' was hammered out, perhaps over a long period of time, and Nedham when drafting the 'Letter' copied out some of his neatest sentences from it.[35]

Both works, it is to be remembered, were dealing with a

topic of the utmost sensitivity. They were intrusions into the field of high politics, where insignificant merchants ventured at their peril. Certainly there is no evidence that the production of the 'Book' landed Nedham in any trouble – too many important people, from Secretary Cecil downwards, were in agreement with him. But neither does it seem that the 'Book' bore any immediate fruit; indeed, whether the queen ever cast an eye on it is not known. It is perhaps significant that while Nedham made no secret of his authorship of the 'Book' and divulged his name on the first page, he was subsequently always careful to keep out of the limelight – so much so, in fact that his responsibility for the 'Letter', which cannot reasonably be doubted, has hitherto never been asserted. Of course, his friends in the City must have been aware that he harboured a searching political vision and was a sharp critic of the continued reliance on the Antwerp mart; but once he had returned to mind his business in the Netherlands it would hardly have been wise for him to open his mouth much on such a topic. However, he prudently maintained a footing in England, where in December 1562 he took up a lease of some former monastic property at Corsham in Wiltshire, paying an entry fine of a hundred marks (£66 13*s* 4*d*) and settling with the royal exchequer for an annual rent of £27 6*s* 8*d* in addition.[36] He already had an interest in the mining ventures of the entrepreneur Thomas Thurland, as whose creditor for a couple of hundred pounds he appeared in 1561; ultimately, when in 1568 Thurland's Company of Mines Royal was floated, Nedham was listed among the smallest investors as owner of a modest quarter-share.[37]

Meanwhile, the accustomed trade between London and the Netherlands continued to flourish until the middle of 1563. In the summer and autumn of that year, London was devastated by a severe visitation of the plague, with an unprecedented loss of life. There was a resultant delay in the departure of the autumn cloth-fleet for Antwerp. Using the incidence of the plague as a pretext, the Regent of the Netherlands in November mischievously forbade the import of English-made cloths, thereby confronting the merchants of London with the disagreeable choice between either financial disaster or discovering a new market.[38] She also unwittingly provided Nedham with the opportunity of a lifetime. He grasped it with both hands, to revive and re-state the claims of Emden for consideration as a port of entry to the continent for England in place of Antwerp or anywhere else in the Netherlands: the moment had come for him to set his hand to the 'Letter'. The queen and her privy councillors were closely involved in the sequence of events that marked this major commercial crisis, which was not to be resolved for over a year. At the highest political level, the chief intermediary between the courts of the Queen of England and of the Counts of East Friesland was the venerable humanist Jan Utenhove, now settled at London; but in the practical work of planning the dispatch of the cloth-fleet of the London merchants to Emden, George Nedham soon came to stand beside the Governor of the Merchants Adventurers, John Marsh.

At what point in the winter of 1563–4 Nedham returned to London we do not know. His presence must have been welcome to Governor Marsh and other forward spirits among the Merchants Adventurers who had need of his assurances to blow away the dismal forebodings of Richard Clough, the factor of Sir Thomas Gresham at Antwerp, and the other timid cloth-dealers who dreaded the thought of cutting English foreign trade away from its ancient moorings in the Netherlands.[39] Nedham was certainly among the advance party of cloth exporters who on 6 April 1564 sailed from the Thames in order to see to the administrative arrangements requisite at Emden for the reception of the main cloth-fleet. A week later, he was writing to let Secretary Cecil know that they had safely made the port. Indeed, the navigation had proved much easier than he had feared, so that 'with very little exercise a simple mariner shall be able to bring a good ship thither': his previous visit or visits had evidently been overland. The news that the English would shortly hold their mart at Emden had been received, as he put it, 'with no small rejoicing' by the townsfolk as well as by the Counts of East Friesland, and he was able to report that 'all things we have asked is [*sic*] granted us'.[40] It must be mentioned that there was a less fervent appraisal of the situation by another member of the English delegation, whose opinion is on record: he certainly confirmed the enthusiasm of the burghers and the Counts, and added that communications with the interior of Germany were as good as those from Antwerp. But he noted a possible scarcity of packhouses for storing the English cloths, and also of lodging-houses; the town struck him as waterlogged, and the local currency was 'base', though fortunately Netherlands coins freely circulated.[41]

The main cloth-fleet sailed in May, arriving without serious mishap at Emden by the 23rd. There was, from the outset, a lack of southern wares to buy for the English market, though for a time there were brisk sales of English woollen cloths. But in mid-July business dried up – the boycott of Emden organised at the instigation of the government at Brussels had proved all too effective. Ultimately, the Englishmen found that by undertaking the transport of their cloths overland to Frankfurt-am-Main it was practicable at fair-time in the autumn to renew contact with the German commodity market, though the journey was wearisome, risky and expensive. But the misery wrought at Antwerp by the absence of English cloths was proving even more painful, especially because it coincided with a shortage of corn owing to an interruption of supplies from the Baltic.[42] It was therefore the Regent of the Netherlands and not the Queen of England who had first to climb down. A new Spanish ambassador arrived during June at the English royal court, and negotiations for ending the trade rupture before long were set in hand. The Emden mart had not been anything like a full success for the English, and doubtless most City merchants felt greatly relieved when it was called off; but politically the English had gained a tactical advantage, evident when the Regent of the Netherlands ceased to insist upon the terms she had been seeking at the beginning of the year.

It is with this sequence of events in mind, as they took place in the course of the year 1564, that the 'Letter to the Earls of East Friesland' must be read. George Nedham was prominent among the little group of Londoners who defiantly welcomed the breach with Antwerp. They comprised a minority, perhaps a small minority, in the City. They were resolute, protestant in sympathy, anti-Spanish and so by implication anti-Netherlands in outlook; they put their ideals before their immediate profit. Their leader was John Marsh, for many years Governor of the Merchants Adventurers; their best-known other personalities a little later were to be enumerated by the Spanish ambassador in England as Alderman Lionel Duckett and four other merchants adventurers of whom one was Thomas Aldersey, who had served as Deputy Governor of the Fellowship at Emden when the cloth-fleet arrived there; George Nedham was another.[43] We may imagine the fierce exchange of arguments in the City during the year. But it was the moderate majority whose will prevailed. The English government not surprisingly responded affirmatively to the overtures of the Spanish ambassador; after all, it was anxious not only to restore industrial activity in the clothmaking regions but also to collect its vital customs revenue at London. So it carried through the necessary negotiations and brought about the resumption of normal traffic with Antwerp and the Netherlands from the first day of January 1565.

For Nedham and his friends, the return of the cloth traffic to Antwerp at the beginning of January 1565 was a discouraging and damaging event. As a result of the misfiring of the Emden mart, the 'Letter' must have seemed to lose most of its point before it was even complete. Some of his bitterness is to be felt in the language of the introduction, presumably prefixed at a late stage to the text of the 'Letter', where he fulminates against Spanish influence in German affairs. Its toleration in 1564, he states, 'was not only a foul dishonour' but also a political peril, suggestive of an indifference on the part of the German ruling princes towards the disasters of their neighbours – as if 'seeing your neighbour's house afire, ye took no care for your own.'[44] As he dolefully predicted, before long, all from 'the highest prince to the poorest ploughman in Germany should feel the smart'. Nedham himself performed one final and melancholy office in January 1565 at Emden, by presiding as Deputy Governor over the winding-up of the English mercantile settlement there. A farewell dinner was offered to the Burgomasters and Town Councillors, and Nedham sent a message of thanks to the Counts of East Friesland, asking them not to speak ill of the English merchants until they had heard from the queen and the Fellowship by letter.[45]

Meanwhile, Nedham was confronted by a new personal problem. With the re-opening of the trade to the Netherlands, other men might return to their old haunts and resume their former livelihood, but not 'the discoverer of Emden'. He did not dare to show his face again at Antwerp. As a stop-gap, in 1565 and subsequent years, he found some employment at the hands of the Anglo-German copper-mining enterprise that eventually took shape as the Company of Mines Royal. On its behalf, he toiled to Wales and Ireland in search of supplies of timber to be used in the smelting process as fuel. He also travelled to the Lake District, where he suspected the rustic inhabitants to be treasonably inclined. Here he conducted negotiations on behalf of the Company with the Earl of Northumberland, owner of the mineral rights in which the mining associates were interested, and generally at other times made himself useful.[46] When in May 1568 the Company received its royal charter, George Nedham, as we have seen, was included among the twenty-three shareholders, though as one of the smallest proprietors.[47] It is evident from his letters that he spent many weeks, if not months, in the North of England during 1567 and 1568. However, these were activities that bore little upon the topics with which the 'Letter to the Earls of East Friesland' was concerned, and it is not necessary to dwell upon them here. But it may be noted that they brought him from time to time into contact with Secretary Cecil and some other personages of high political importance.

However, service with the Company of Mines Royal may not have been particularly remunerative. Certainly Nedham did not feel that it relieved him from the need to find a living by some other means. He had, after all, some claim upon the gratitude of the government. Secretary Cecil and other influential Privy Councillors were aware of his services, and Cecil had even seen the text of the 'Letter'.[48] But how was Nedham to be employed? An obvious answer was provided by the London customs administration, the source of the greater part of the royal revenue and believed to be in need of an overhaul. It was probably now that, at the instance of

Secretary Cecil, Nedham was taken into unofficial or semi-official service by the old Lord Treasurer Winchester to check the payment of customs duties by the merchants at London – in Nedham's words, 'I was called and commanded to travail in these matters of custom paying'.[49] Further, the Queen was induced to promise him the reversion of the farm of the Custom House quay, the chief landing-place at the Port of London, which in time should yield him a competence.[50] A further approach to the Queen *c.* 1567 was met by the grant of a right to levy cranage and lighterage dues upon half the woollen cloths and fine wares passing through the Custom House for shipment or landing:[51] between them these categories covered most of the wares in transit through London.

But alas, these well-meant efforts by Nedham's patrons failed to yield him the security he sought. The queen, who on a later occasion is known to have insisted upon the retention of an unofficial watchdog at Thames-side landing places, doubtless gave him her support.[52] But the old Lord Treasurer did not like snoopers and was a lukewarm friend. As early as September 1565, he was keeping Nedham waiting for his authorisation.[53] From the exchequer, Winchester viewed Nedham as a somewhat unreliable character, 'a man that forgetteth all payment'.[54] Nedham's fortunes indeed sank to a low point in the mid-1560s. In or about 1568, and evidently in desperation, he poured out his troubles to the Earl of Leicester at the prompting, as he alleged, of the retired soldier and diplomat Sir William Pickering.[55] There was a whole catalogue of setbacks and disappointments to rehearse. He had exhausted his capital and lost 'credit, estimation and friends' at both London and Antwerp. His career as a merchant had been terminated five years earlier, with the rupture of trade relations with the Netherlands in 1563, since when his employment at London in connection with the customs had earned him 'such evil will amongst all merchants both English and strangers' that any return to business there was out of the question. He was still afraid to return to his old haunts at Antwerp, where there clung to him the dangerous reputation of being 'the first inventor and discloser of Emden'; his wife's friends had warned him that he stood in great personal peril were he to show his face again at Antwerp. His negotations with the Lord Treasurer for a lease of the farm of the cranes and the new wharf projected at London had not yet led anywhere. He was aware of how 'it is thought by many and spoken of some, that I have beat(en) the bush and other men shall have the birds'. 'Surely', he wrote, 'of necessity I must be forced to leave London and go into the country; for in London I cannot live with quietness and to Antwerp I dare not go'.

However, a serious rift in Anglo-Netherlands relations was now imminent, and with it some improvement in the prospects of George Nedham. Near the end of December 1568, all English merchants in the Netherlands were arrested by order of the Spanish viceroy Alva. There was immediate retaliation in kind by the Queen of England, and all commercial links between London and Antwerp were *ipso facto* again sundered, this time for five years. During this period, the cloth fleets of the Merchants Adventurers sailed to Hamburg instead of Antwerp: to make for Emden was judged unsafe owing to the presence of a garrison of Spanish troops at Delfzijl on the other side of the river Ems, though English relations with Emden and the rulers of East Friesland continued to be cordial.[56] The points set forth in 'A Letter to the Earls of East Friesland' about the political disadvantage of Antwerp suddenly became germane once more to the current situation. The copy of the 'Letter' (only one existed) was unearthed and discreetly brought to the remembrance of Secretary Cecil in March 1569, with a suggestion that it might interest the queen herself, and an apology that it was 'not so well handled in the writing as the state of the prince and the matter requireth'.[57] But in fact the sentiments chimed harmoniously with the anti-Spanish feeling now predominant at the royal court, where the 'Letter' now circulated among the privy councillors. Nedham was actually allowed to defend his opinions before them, and 'he departed with victory'. It was further alleged, with perhaps only a little exaggeration, that the queen herself was 'longing to see him'. When two months later the letter was returned, it was with a direction to show it to Governor Marsh of the

Merchants Adventurers and to Thomas Aldersey, who had served as Deputy Governor at Emden in 1564.[58]

In the ensuing years, the international situation was slow to improve. The cessation of trade between England and the Netherlands can only have bettered the standing of Nedham and made his arguments seem the more relevant and attractive. At the royal court, his most faithful friend seems to have remained Secretary Cecil, though at the Council table he had supporters in Sir Francis Knollys and Sir Walter Myldmay, among others.[59] In the City he might count upon the backing of Governor Marsh, Thomas Aldersey and doubtless other good protestants. The death of the old Lord Treasurer Winchester in March 1572 was indirectly of advantage to him. Certainly it was in the following month that Nedham approached Cecil, now Lord Burghley, with the proposal that he might revise and translate the 'Letter' into Low German – 'the doche tongue' – and present it personally and privately to the Earls in East Friesland 'as a token of my good will always borne towards them and their country'.[60] This was in fact done, though without producing any result.[61] But for Nedham the most decisive event occurred in July that year, when after a period of hesitation the queen promoted Burghley to the vacant Lord Treasurership. Nedham's chief patron was now in a position where he could be of much more use to him. Early in September, the survival of the 'Letter' was much brightened when several further copies were made and, presumably, distributed.[62]

All these developments signified so many breaks in the clouds for Nedham. Already during the lifetime of the old Lord Treasurer he had devised a scheme for 'redress of the misorders' at the London Custom House. Winchester had long cherished a project for enlarging the wharfage area to deal with the greatly increased volume of traffic converging upon it, building a new Custom House and in general minimising the loss of revenue for which the customs officers were suspected of being responsible. Nedham had characteristically 'drawn out a book' which he had shown to Secretary Cecil, who told him to submit it to the Lord Treasurer. Winchester had approved the sketch and ordered him to proceed with the detailed surveys, indicating where warehouses, cranes and offices might be erected.[63] Nedham's intention, that space should be provided to enable all commodities in transit to be 'laden and unladen at the same place, in the sight and presence of Her Majesty's officers and other people that be bystanders' and not at dark or private holes and corners on 'blind quays', tallied with the aims Winchester had tried to achieve in 1559, when he had been empowered by statute to establish the requisite measures.[64] There had been further attempted reforms in 1564, but their execution had been hampered by the still inadequate wharfage and buildings. The old Lord Treasurer had 'of late years' grown blind to the corruptions of the customs officers 'who in manner did what they would without controlment', amassing for themselves marvellous and unprecedented great wealth. The head officers, Nedham alleged, merely appeared at the quayside for a couple of hours in the morning, leaving the conduct of official business to their clerks and other underlings. In his judgment, 'the greatest deceit and damage that is or hath been done to Her Majesty is by the consent and procurement of her own officers . . . and specially by the under-officers as waiters, searchers and customers' clerks', whose 'many delays' and 'cunning and subtle fetches' resulted in both the defrauding of the crown and the oppression of the merchants.[65]

Now, with a younger and far more vigorous Lord Treasurer, the hour seemed to have arrived for some thoroughgoing changes. Nedham certainly had a clear and business-like grasp of the reforms needed at the London Custom House. Since it was here that most of the crown revenue was generated, his proposals were certain of attention if he had the ear of the Lord Treasurer. Central to his plan was the enlargement of the Custom House and its wharf, as he had urged it upon old Winchester some years before. Within the new buildings, there were to be two convenient but separate places for checking merchandise, one inward, one outward. With an efficient registration system, and the regular attendance of the customs officers at their appointed hours, their staff might be drastically reduced and purged of untrustworthy underlings, to the great benefit of the royal revenue. Some of the abusive practices of the merchants he explained in detail. But with regard to the misdeeds of the officials he limited himself mostly to generalisations, though he offered some revelations by word of mouth. His boldest sally was the dark hint that 'there be many that do mislike and think dangerous that Mr Birde', responsible for collecting the crucial cloth export tax at London, should have as his Comptroller his brother-in-law the Merchant Adventurer William Revett. 'For they two agreeing, may do much harm divers ways'. He recommended that every office-holder in the Customs should annually make an appearance before the Lord Treasurer in the Court of Exchequer, 'and there openly to stand and answer for any wrongs that may be objected against him, either on Her Majesty's behalf or on behalf of the merchants and shippers as well English as strangers', on pain of having his tenure terminated. Nedham thought the customs officials were a poor lot, and he believed that 'without some sharp and severe order they will not be reformed'.[66]

Such zeal was dangerous. Nedham did not fail to be aware of the many enemies he was raising. As he put it, 'I have made of my friends my enemies, who cease not both with foul words and other indirect means both to hinder me but also overthrow my proceedings, which I shall not be able to follow unless Her Highness and [her *sc.*] honourable Council stand with me in this honest service towards Her Majesty'.[67] He needed support both authoritative and material. The reversionary right to the farm of the Custom House quays had not yet fallen to him. And the right to levy cranage and lighterage dues upon half the wares in transit there had proved a sad disappointment: the grant had proved bothersome and ultimately impracticable to enforce, so deep was the ill-will of the quay-keepers, and the profit had been 'very little'. To add to his troubles, his house at Bergen-op-Zoom was 'utterly spoiled and broken down', and his lands and tenements in Holland 'so wasted by the civil and intestine wars in that country that the tenants be driven from their farms, wherby no rent be paid'.[68] Nedham wielded sufficient influence to have this grievance ventilated to the Netherlands envoys visiting London in March 1574. But they dismissed it as an incident 'in the calamity of war, from which the houses and goods of Englishmen cannot be exempt any more than others'.[69]

Nedham, now over fifty years of age, and by the standards of the time an old man, was rescued from his distress by the Lord Treasurer. Burghley in December 1577 made up his mind that he should at last have the farm of the Custom House quay.[70] He was to pay an annual rent of £40, 'and be bound unto all reparations, and to erect divers new buildings'. In return, he might expect to receive the payment of cranage and wharfage dues from merchants making use of the landing-place. In view, as it was phrased, 'of his long expectation', he lease was made out to George Nedham and his son Arthur 'for the term of the longer liver of them'.[71] Henceforth, he was established in a position of central importance to the customs administration of the Port of London, where he soon proved himself a stubborn defender of his rights. In 1565, a regulation had been framed to ensure that woollen cloths, and all fine wares and haberdashery wares, should be laden or discharged at the Custom House quay only. These were the commodities attracting almost all the customs duties, and likely to provide most of the money the quay-keeper might expect to collect. But the 1565 rules had for some years not been fully enforced, and Nedham soon found that his rights as the new farmer of this pre-eminent quay were being challenged by the keepers of the other riverside quays, his envious rivals. He appealed to his patron the Lord Treasurer, who appointed his henchmen Peter Osborne and Thomas Fanshawe of the Exchequer to enquire into the situation. Their verdict was clear. They advised that the 1565 regulation should once more be enforced, since it provided the only means to ensure that inspection of wares was public; they added that if the Custom House quay proved inconveniently small, then the more or less disused 'Old Wool Quay' nearby might be added to it.[72] With this support, Nedham in his last years was able to battle against the pretensions of his rivals the other quay-keepers.[73]

He died in 1584, intestate.[74] His son Francis was a little later acting as one of the continental agents of Secretary Walsingham, and subsequently served with Leicester in the Netherlands.[75] Arthur, the other son, was still in charge of the Custom

House quay in 1596, when the upper rooms of the official building were in use as his dwelling-place.[76] He was to survive until 1603.[77] One of his sons, baptised George after the grandfather, graduated in 1604 from Christ Church, Oxford, and followed a career in holy orders, holding livings in Surrey and Sussex.[78] The family thus exemplified a certain degree of both social and geographical mobility. This was especially true of old George, for the country lad from Snitterton had come far. His rustic upbringing in Derbyshire had been followed by travels that at one time or another took him to Wales and Ireland and on the continent to places as far afield as Emden and probably Venice. Also, he had become a freeman of the City of London, he had habituated himself to the ways of the commercial metropolis of Antwerp, and he had acquired marriage-ties as well as property in the Netherlands. He had brought himself favourably to the notice of the ruling personages of his native land; most notably, he had won and kept the confidence of Lord Treasurer Burghley. He remained aware of how his education had indeed been, to use his own favourite description, 'rude', but he knew how to express himself in prose that was clear and pungent (even if occasionally weak in grammar), and he had enough native wit to comprehend the springs of action, political and economic, that animated the men among whom his life was cast; and he had left some memorials of his thought for later generations to ponder.

III
A tract for the times

'A Letter to the Earls of East Friesland' is a treatise of some 36,000 words, addressed to the brothers who had inherited the right to rule in this small principality of the Holy Roman Empire lying on the North Sea coast, ostensibly by a subject of theirs. Nowhere is the name of the writer stated, though four of the nine surviving copies indicate his initials, W.G. In all likelihood, these were intended to suggest as author the elderly scholar and schoolmaster Wilhelm Gnapheus, who on at least a couple of occasions had visited London as the accredited agent of the East Friesland princes and must therefore have been to some extent known in the City. Gnapheus had leanings in religion which in 1530 had forced him to forsake his native Netherlands, and his life subsequently had been spent in Prussia and East Friesland, which he had eulogised in a Latin poem printed in 1557. He had also acquired some fame as author of *Akolastus*, a play after the manner of Terence.[79] On a superficial view, the ascription of the 'Letter' to Gnapheus has attractions, but it is inconceivable that in fact he could have written it, if only because it is most unlikely that he had the requisite command of English or the commercial knowledge it displays; in any case, he died in 1568, and therefore could not have written the author's postscript, dated 1572.

As to the relationship of Nedham and Gnapheus, it is not easy to step beyond the morass of conjecture. Certainly there had been some communication between England and East Friesland in the 1550s, based on ecclesiastical affinities, and it is known that before the year 1564 Gnapheus had for some time been advising the East Friesland princes and their mother the Countess Anna in their relations with the Queen of England.[80] Towards the end of 1562, Gnapheus had himself been in London on their behalf, seeking to induce the Merchants Adventurers to set up a subsidiary mart at Emden.[81] It was, of course, precisely the purpose of Nedham when he wrote his 'Book' to commend the forging of such a link, and to assure the Queen of England that any diplomatic advance on her part would meet with a warm response.[82] It is hard to believe that at this stage Nedham and Gnapheus had not met, whether at Emden, London or both. As we have seen, the origins of the 'Letter' follow closely upon the completion of the 'Book', which may have been as late as 1563.[83] 'Letter' and 'Book' are complementary and overlapping documents: the 'Book' being written from a frankly English point of view, while the 'Letter' puts the arguments that should appeal to the rulers of East Friesland. This is particularly true of the first twenty-five articles, which explain how precarious the great wealth of Antwerp and the Netherlands really is. When in November 1563 the Regent of the Netherlands rashly brought about a formal cessation of trade with England, the hour had struck for George Nedham. For the commercial crisis now overhanging the City, he had a remedy. One set of arguments he had thought out and committed to paper in the 'Book', and now – it might be suggested – he began seriously to frame its counterpart the 'Letter'. At the same time, the Merchants Adventurers were groping towards a resolution to fix their cloth mart at Emden, a decision ratified by the queen and her Council on 21 or 22 January 1564. By then, some part of the 'Letter' had probably been drafted.

Meanwhile, arrangements had been put in hand for the dispatch of a couple of London merchants to ascertain the attitude of the East Friesland rulers to the project of establishing an English cloth mart at Emden. Nedham was accredited as one of them to the Countess Anna and her sons on 18 January; it may be assumed that the pair set sail with the first favourable wind following the decision of the Privy Council three or four days later.[84] Before long, he was doubtless in contact with Gnapheus on East Friesland soil. The Countess and her sons proved welcoming, and they in turn dispatched three envoys, of whom Gnapheus was one, to London to conclude a detailed agreement with the English. The delegation sailed from Emden on 22 February, and so was presumably in London by the end of the month.[85] Perhaps Nedham accompanied them, though on this point there is no evidence; but he was certainly back in London before long. He then sailed again with the advance-party of merchants for Emden on 6 April.[86] Amid all this coming and going, Nedham and Gnapheus may well have been thrown together a good deal during the first three months of 1564. However, as Gnapheus and his colleagues brought with them in February the general consent of the Counts of East Friesland to the project of organising an English cloth mart at Emden, the composition of a letter recommending the Merchants Adventurers to them must have lost the urgency it had previously possessed in the eyes of Nedham. Besides, in March both Gnapheus and Nedham were occupied with public business: Gnapheus in conducting his negotiations for the detailed arrangements at the mart, while being feted in the City; and Nedham must have been drawn increasingly into the practical preparations for the departure of the cloth-ships with which he was to travel.[87] Whatever fragment of the 'Letter' had been drafted is likely to have been laid aside.

Then for months rather than weeks the unfinished 'Letter' was neglected. It must have been late in summer when Nedham again took up the fragment. The evidence of articles thirty-five and sixty suffices to indicate how deeply provoked he felt by the success of the Netherlands government in fending off the great international trade firms from attendance at the Emden mart. It was on or about 22 May that the edict in the name of Philip II forbidding trade with Emden or the English was published in the various provinces of the Netherlands; and by mid-July there was visible and painful proof that – in conjunction with political pressure applied elsewhere – it was achieving its purpose. In response to this setback, Nedham resumed his pen and drafted articles twenty-six to thirty-nine, denouncing the unconstitutional interference of Philip of Spain with German liberties as exemplified by the malicious smothering of the English cloth mart. Nedham next proceeded to set forth a careful account of the nature of the traffic in semi-manufactured woollen cloths and the need for labour which it generated, and then turned at article sixty to address himself to the princes of Germany, seeking to explain to them why they must unite and stand firm against the ill-omened 'great league and friendship' that linked King Philip and the Pope.[88] Very revealingly, his sources led him to accept that Philip was personally 'a gentle and merciful prince, inclined to all peace and quietness', but tethered to papal policy by his political needs in Italy. The real villain of the piece was the Pope 'and his shavelings', scheming how they might set up 'all Christendom through their popish and bloody kingdom again'.[89] Evidently George Nedham stood on the same side of the ecclesiastical fence as that other London merchant, Henry Brinklow, who in 1548 had put forth the scarifying *Complaynt of Roderyck Mors*.

Nedham finally rounded off the 'Letter' by an account of Anglo-Burgundian relations during the previous seventy years – the point being to demonstrate what valuable friends the kings of England had proved. However, there was always a tendency for Nedham in this section rather to stress how the

English had been left in the lurch by their allies the dukes of Burgundy – a line of argument that he had already pursued more briefly in the 'Book'.[90] The reader may feel that at this stage the pretence of writing for the Counts of East Friesland was wearing thin. It may well be that in the autumn of 1564 Nedham was back in England, where he would have heard gloomy tidings of the incipient rapprochement with the King of Spain and his Regent in the Netherlands. He refers on various occasions to the summer as a season that is past.[91] There shone a tardy ray of light with the news that the patricians of Bruges were actually trying to tempt the English merchants back to their own city – the reference being to a couple of letters to Secretary Cecil, dated 2 and 4 December, one from the Count of Egmont, Governor of Flanders, and the other from the municipality of Bruges.[92] But the last touches to the 'Letter' are likely to have been added before or not long after Christmas, since in January 1565 Nedham was momentarily back at Emden, and filling the office of Deputy Governor of the Merchants Adventurers there.[93]

Probably at this point the 'Letter' was shown to Secretary Cecil, who may well have approved of the contents, but not to the point of encouraging publication.[94] Nedham, who had put all his knowledge and judgement into the effort of composition, may equally well have been disappointed, but his feelings are not on record. The interest of the text lies in part in the way it mirrors the responses of a freeman of the City of London to a series of pressures, commercial and political, as they bore upon him during twelve eventful months. The obscurities are due partly to the change in his motives during this period. Originally, it is to be inferred, he was expecting to have the 'Letter' turned into Low German for presentation by Gnapheus to the Counts of East Friesland, and he wrote as if he were a subject of theirs. But when he resumed work on it perhaps in the late summer, he can hardly have thought of the 'Letter' as merely for transmission abroad, however close his contacts with Gnapheus. His analysis of the economy of the Netherlands, and even his survey of the overweening influence of Philip II in Germany conveyed a lesson that concerned his fellow-countrymen almost as much as the princes of Germany; in article thirty-nine, where he dilated upon the danger of allowing merchants to marry foreign women – as he himself had done – he was touching upon an issue much to the fore among the merchants adventurers of the City at the time.[95] In the final articles, written probably late in the year, the tendency to look at the world frankly as an Englishman is apparent. Nedham was no longer simply seeking to promote a single specific issue but setting forth his views on some general topics, writing a major disquisition upon the international politics and commerce of north-western Europe, a tract for the times – and incidentally marking a step forward in the writing of descriptive economics.

If we agree that in the course of drafting the 'Letter' Nedham changed his mind and dropped his original idea of getting his friend Gnapheus to present a translation to the Counts of East Friesland, a further question arises. Why did he not complete the transformation, end the disguise and with it the ascription of authorship to 'W.G.'? To his friends and patrons it can have been no secret that it was he, George Nedham, who was composing or had composed the 'Letter'. Poor Nedham was always conscious of his meagre literary education, of how 'my phrase be but rude and my style but tedious, for lack of that skill that a man meanly learned might easily mend'.[96] To any knowing person he could hardly have hoped to pass off his prose, even in translation, as the product of so celebrated and polished a humanist writer as Gnapheus. But the simple fact that Philip II was still the political ally of the queen would have made any advertisement of his authorship unwise. Besides, there was now a new and effective Spanish ambassador at the royal court, with an inquisitive eye for heretics and other enemies of his master among the London merchants.[97] It would thus have been highly imprudent for Nedham, a property-owner in the Netherlands, gratuitously to publicise his activities. So the initials of Wilhelm Gnapheus, originally used as part of the scheme for delivering the 'Letter' overseas, acquired a new utility. They served as a convenient smoke-screen for the statement of Nedham's opinions. The cover was ingenious and plausible. Any busybody could learn about Gnapheus in the City or at the royal court; but to verify the identification would have been perplexing and probably impracticable for the casual enquirer.

Nedham wrote the 'Letter' because he believed in the cause it was intended to foster. Of course, he had supporters, from Secretary Cecil downwards, who gave him at least some encouragement. But, as we have seen, his advocacy of the Emden mart brought him nothing but personal hardship. He was not so simple as to be unaware of the obloquy he was likely to bring upon himself, which was doubtless why he liked to keep his name hidden. The 'Letter', it may be recalled, was neither his first nor his last intervention in the field of public policy. Its prose is marked by occasional flashes of style that indicate how his literary gifts, had they received further training, might have enabled him to make a name for his pen; we may guess that Nedham was by temperament a compulsive writer, in his way a forerunner of Edward Misselden or even Daniel Defoe. But in the end it was doubtless his ardour as a patriot and a protestant that counted. To promote a cause rather than make a name for himself was his ambition. In this, as in other ways, he resembled his remarkable but anonymous predecessor the author of *The Libelle of Englyshe Polycye*, who had treated comparable topics a mere three or four generations previously.[98] Or, alternatively, he might be compared with his successor the seventeenth-century merchant Thomas Mun, who too had a cause to uphold and a large field to survey; but *England's Treasure by Forraign Trade* remained sufficiently valid, forty years after it had been written, to be printed and published entire, while within the same space of time the world known to George Nedham had vanished.

Probably the least interesting and certainly the least original portions of the 'Letter' are those where Nedham was relying upon his book learning: *i.e.*, where he was peering into events too early or too recondite to be familiar to contemporaries. For happenings in western Europe during the previous generation or so, he relied upon the *Chronicles* of John Carion, of which an English translation had been published in 1550; he also drew upon John Sleidan's *Chronicle* or *Commentaries*, the English translation of which appeared ten years later.[99] He does not divulge the names of the 'other ancient writers' from whom he took his knowledge of German medieval history and of Anglo-Burgundian relations in the fifteenth century. It is unlikely that his reading was very wide; though there is an airy reference to Aristotle and Theophrastus, ignorance of Latin probably precluded much investigation.[100] By the standards of his age, Nedham knew himself to be an unlettered man. Of how to construct sentences even in his native language he was none too sure – at times, the main verb becomes buried in the sand of a succession of subordinate clauses, or verb and subject fail to agree in number or person. It was a very exceptional merchant indeed – Richard Hilles, merchant adventurer and freeman of the Merchant Taylors' Company of London, among Nedham's contemporaries comes to mind – who could both pursue trade and maintain some foothold in the world of learning.

However, for any lack of book-learning there is ample compensation in the characteristic instruments of the merchant – observation and argument, always two powerful agents in the march of civilization.[101] Thus when Nedham visited the Westphalian town of Lingen he used the opportunity to listen to the officers of the German mercenaries holding the place for the King of Spain, and was able to note the rumour that 'a strong castle' was to be built there. He had no difficulty in appreciating the significance of this.[102] But the most fruitful field for his comments was offered by the Netherlands. He did not, indeed, foresee the coming deluge of the Revolt and the Eighty Years' War, soon to transform the map of north-west Europe. In his eyes, the seventeen provinces ruled by the House of Burgundy were simply the embodiment of an economic miracle – they were 'countries that of themselves be barren' but that had marvellously 'gotten and daily do get great riches' and had become the seat of 'great number of strong and fair cities, which are become very populous and full of rich merchants'.[103] Their inhabitants, he thought, were unwarlike and 'be no good soldiers', a remark that events were soon to belie.[104] With more prescience he noted the decay of German national feeling in the Netherlands – 'the people said they were King Philip's subjects and under the House of Burgundy, and almost think it a scorn to be called

German or imperial, and specially the youth'.[105] It was an attitude symptomatic of the new Dutch nationalism that was moving towards its birth.

In the finances of the Netherlands government Nedham felt a special interest. No doubt he wrote with some feeling the remark that the province of Holland had lost its freedom in 1552, when its inhabitants were first compelled to pay the taxes known as the Tenth and Twentieth Penny 'both against the law, and also the promise and oath of the Emperor and King Philip his son'.[106] Being a property-owner in that province, through his wife, he was personally affected. As to the total yield of the Tenth and Twentieth Penny, which he reckoned to have been levied ten times during the years 1546–60, plus the receipts from a Benevolence and from Chimney Money, he was able to state figures doubtless obtained from knowledgeable friends on the Antwerp Bourses.[107] From these, he was in a position to infer that the Netherlands represented for the Emperor Charles V and his son Philip II of Spain a possession more valuable than the Indies East and West. Indeed, his reflections led him further still, to the radical conclusion that since the Indies produced merely 'a little gold and silver', all too dearly bought by the death and blood of so many Christian people, and on the other hand absorbed so many 'necessary things, both victuals and needful commodities' as to lead to 'a general dearth and scarceness of the same to be . . . here in Christendom', 'it were not amiss if that trade into the Indies were clean left off'. The Spaniards should therefore follow the example of the ancient Carthaginians and wind up their ventures to America, whose gold and silver 'is in one prince's hand, and partly too the occasion of all the war and trouble that hath been in Christendom this forty or fifty years'.[108]

Oral history has its pitfalls. Nedham's statements about fifteenth-century Antwerp are somewhat wide of the mark. Certainly the rise of Antwerp was a phenomenon of the later middle ages; certainly, it displaced Bruges as the chief commercial centre of north-west Europe; certainly, the advent of the English merchants was vital for its continued progress.[109] But long before 1500 it was a haunt of international trade and a financial resort of increasing importance, particularly while the Fairs of Brabant were in swing, and known to the English as a good market. The progress of Antwerp had its ups and downs, but the brief period of world-famous brilliance in the sixteenth century was in prospect considerably before 1494, Nedham's date for its inception.[110] Already in the 1470s there were some sixty sea-going ships of Antwerp, from the Baltic to the Mediterranean, on the waters at any given moment.[111] The 'old men yet living' whom Nedham 'heard say' that at the first coming of the English there were not in all Antwerp above four merchants were recounting a tall story.[112] It contains a core of truth, in that the rise of Antwerp was in its early phase marked by the activity of the inland traders from Cologne, Aachen and elsewhere in Germany, the overseas merchants lingering for some years at Bruges. But the attraction of the Fairs of Brabant, to which the prosperity of Antwerp was always linked, may be traced back to the fourteenth century and even earlier. The first settlement of the English cloth exporters dates from at least the middle decades of the fifteenth century, while the English were selling their wool at Antwerp much earlier still.[113]

It is when Nedham comes to describe Antwerp as he himself knows it that the historical value of the 'Letter' is strongest. The classic portrayal of Antwerp in its heyday was written by the Florentine merchant Ludovico Guicciardini in 1560 but first printed only in 1567; it is thus not specially likely that Nedham was acquainted with it, though he may well have met its author.[114] The fact that the two men substantially concur in their account of the metropolis of commerce need however indicate no more than that each knew what he was describing and faithfully restricted himself to the facts. Of course, Nedham's Antwerp was not that of Guicciardini, though both had an interest in the commodity trade. The Englishman exhibited a closer concern with exact figures, though the sweep of his information was narrower than that of Guicciardini. The Florentine tells us more about the daily life of the merchant and the world of high finance; Nedham refers only briefly, and seemingly with disapproval, to the entry of Netherlands merchants into the business of international currency 'exchange and delivering money by interest or, to term it plainly, by usury'.[115] Moral objections to the practice hardly weighed at all with the merchant habituated to the advanced financial techniques of his fellow-Italians. But Nedham's dislike was reinforced by political reasoning, in that the growth of the Antwerp money market made it easier for the ruler of the Netherlands to raise capital to finance his military preparations.[116]

Nedham's strong point, as might be expected of an experienced dealer in textiles, lay in his knowledge of the international traffic in English woollen cloths.[117] He had good reason to dwell on the topic, since the argument that the basic stimulus to the economy of the Netherlands had been supplied by the transit trade in semi-manufactured English textiles was an issue central to the purpose of the 'Letter'. His quantitative estimates are not seriously out of harmony with those of modern historians who have investigated the subject with the added advantage of an acquaintance with the surviving customs records. Nedham estimated the number of cloths shipped each year from England, by merchants both native and foreign, at eighty thousand white and forty thousand coloured. It was a shrewd guess: Nedham's figures were not implausible, though they are no more meaningful than might be expected of averages. If we interpret them as total shipments of 'short cloths' according to the legal definition of these (each equivalent to three kerseys) they may be compared with the numbers returned by the English customs officers for the two fiscal years (Michaelmas to Michaelmas) between the conclusion of international peace in the spring of 1559 and the outbreak of civil war in France in April 1562: for the year 1559–60, such shipments totalled at least 136,121 'short cloths' and for 1560–1 at least 105,553.[118] Unfortunately, it is impossible to discover what proportion (the great majority, fairly certainly) went to the Netherlands and what fraction direct to Spain, France, the Baltic and other markets. However, Guicciardini's estimate that the total value of the English cloths imported each year at Antwerp was as much as five million *écus* is not far distant from Nedham's valuation of those same cloths at £920,000.[119]

Nedham also had a message to deliver about the social consequences of setting up another English cloth mart outside the Netherlands: for one large industrial and labour problem arising out of his project he believed he had an answer. Like others, he was aware of the dependence of many thousands of artisans at Antwerp and elsewhere in the Netherlands upon the traffic with England. At Antwerp alone, the gild of clothworkers – *i.e.*, fullers, shearmen and other finishing specialists – numbered at this time some sixteen hundred members, all dependent for their livelihood upon a supply of English cloths. A further contingent of dependent artificers was represented by the dyers; and there were also the weavers who needed to use English wool, and the artisans who handled the luxury and other goods exported by English merchants.[120] It was commonly believed, as Nedham had often heard it said, that on the English trade there were fed and maintained in the whole Netherlands as many as sixty thousand souls, 'yea, some have said many more'.[121] As to their earnings, Nedham was able to offer an estimate of the total sum yearly gained by Netherlanders 'only by wool and woollen cloth that cometh out of England', which he put at some £600,000.[122] If the English trade in whole or part were lost, this sum would in proportion be forgone and the workfolk with their families cast into distress. There was, in addition, the yield of the taxes collected by the government of the Netherlands from the wares passing to and from England; but no just estimate, he thought, could be made of 'what profit the prince hath by the toll, excises and other duties'.[123]

The problem, as Nedham saw it, lay not at all in the need to provide some sort of succour for the workfolk deprived of their usual employment by the absence of the English merchants and their cloths. His concern pointed in a different direction: to find means of inducing them to migrate to the new mart town selected by the Merchants Adventurers outside the Netherlands. He had practical suggestions to offer. He believed that when the Netherlands clothworkers perceived that the English trade was being diverted to East Friesland, they would naturally be inclined to follow it, and that their migration might be spurred by certain inducements. One such was provided by the lower price-level in East Friesland, where living was cheaper.[124] Another was the freedom from 'unreasonable taxes and payments, such as the Tenth and Twentieth Penny' exacted in the Netherlands.[125] In addition, the immigrant artificer might be encouraged by the grant of a loan to help him establish his new home, as the German cities of Nuremberg and Ulm were wont to make available for the benefit of deserving artisans.[126] But the most ingenious device to be dangled on the word of Nedham was freedom of religion: for the newcomers 'to have liberty openly and freely to use their conscience, and so to instruct and bring up their children and family in the fear of God and the true knowledge of his word and commandments'.[127] The device was in fact to be tried out, with unforeseen results. Antwerp and the Netherlands at this time remained outwardly catholic but reeked of anabaptism and other heresies, to which Calvinism had recently been added; the pastoral care of the clergy at Antwerp was particularly ineffective. Later in the century, there was indeed a migration of artisans from Antwerp and elsewhere to Emden. They carried their beliefs with them, and so Calvinism gained a foothold in the town. The results proved more explosive than Nedham could have dreamt, for ultimately the Counts of East Friesland were to lose their authority over a much more heavily populated Emden, which gained revolutionary autonomy as a city state.[128]

It is impossible to state when Nedham considered he had completed his draft of the 'Letter'. He laid it aside, which is a very different thing, probably very early in 1565, as we have seen.[129] The determining factor was doubtless the decisive victory of the international peacemakers and the joyful resumption of the trade to Antwerp at the beginning of January. The cause he had attempted to sustain in the 'Letter' – as in the 'Book' before it – had received a seemingly fatal rebuff and the incentive to persist had melted away. Besides, he had to look to his own livelihood. He was engaged on work for the customs administration and perhaps already involved in the copper-mining venture promoted by his friend Thomas Thurland and before long to start to travel in its service.[130] His final work on the 'Letter' before the addition of the postscript in

1572 seems to have been to refine and polish, rather than to add new 'articles'. Thus the news of the offer from Bruges to welcome back the Merchants Adventurers, which he cannot have received more than a few days before the end of 1564, was inserted at article one, near the beginning of his text.[131] We might guess that he was considering an improvement to his exposition by casting some of his prose into the form of a dialogue, the fashionable literary contrivance of the age for putting forth and debating new ideas. Nedham may not have read Plato, but he can hardly have been unaware of the achievements of More, Erasmus, Starkey and others in using this device. In eleven of his 'articles' he moved silently into dialogue form, and the editor has therefore inserted the appropriate signs to intimate this to the reader.[132]

IV
The transmission of the text

Nine contemporary manuscript copies of the 'Letter' are known at present to be in existence. There are four in the Department of Manuscripts at the British Library, London, all belonging to different collections; another three are in the Ellesmere manuscript collection at the Huntington Library, San Marino, California; a copy belonging to Earl Fitzwilliam is on deposit at the Northamptonshire Record Office, Delapré Abbey, Northampton; and there is a copy in the Library of the Duke of Northumberland, Alnwick Castle, Northumberland. They vary considerably in presentation, format and even text. None may safely be identified with the original draft as compiled during the twelve months or so ending in early 1565. When in May 1569, after having been seen by Privy Councillors and perhaps the queen, it passed to Governor Marsh of the Merchants Adventurers, it was stated to be 'the only copy remaining abroad'.[133] In all likelihood, it no longer survives.

Nor has it proved possible to locate any copy of the German and Latin translations that without a doubt were made. Since the Counts of East Friesland were presumably ignorant of English, it is easy to understand how Nedham had at the outset intended to make a translation into 'Dutch', *i.e.* Low German.

This at first was an integral part of his project. But in fact it was not achieved until some time after April 1572, thus over seven years after work on the English text had been suspended.[134] This German version was then presented to the three brothers who bore the title of Count of East Friesland; but owing to the fraternal strife dividing them the volume 'rested in their hands and was not preferred', *i.e.* circulated any further.[135] If it still exists, it is presumably in some archive in north-west Germany. There was also a Latin translation, which *c.* 1572–4 remained in the hands of George Nedham, who consulted the Lord Treasurer Burghley about lending it to 'Mr Swartes, who is come hither concerning the mines' – it may be recalled that Nedham and Burghley were both shareholders in the Company of Mines Royal.[136] As to the fate of this Latin version nothing is on record.

List of extant manuscript copies

Symbol	*Location and press-mark*	*Addressee, with date of 1572 postscript*	*Author, if indicated*	*Size, in cms.*
A	Northants R.O. F.(M.) 249	Edzard, John and Christopher 1 September	WG	43.5 × 29
B	BL, Sloane 818	Edzard and John 2 September	–	22.5 × 17
C	BL, Add. 29,251	'My gracious Lord' 2 September	–	22 × 16.5
D	BL, Lansd. 205, ff. 191–233	Edzard and John 1 September	WG	40.9 × 29
E	BL, Add. 48,020, ff. 296–329	'My gracious Lords' 2 September	–	31 × 19
F	Alnwick, MS. 477	Edgerte, John and Christofer 1 September	WG	34 × 23

Symbol	*Location and press-mark*	*Addressee, with date of 1572 postscript*	*Author, if indicated*	*Size, in cms.*
G	Huntington, EL 1604	Lords & States of Empire, & principally the lord of Emden 1 September	–	30 × 19
H	Huntington, EL 1605	Edgert, John and Christopher 2 September	WG	19 × 15
J	Huntington, EL 1606	Lords & States of Empire, & principally the lord of Emden 1 September	–	30 × 21

It may be observed from the table that the nine extant copies of the 'Letter' fall into two distinct groups, differentiated in more ways than one. The first group comprises A, D, F and H, which were all ostensibly copied on the first of September. The five others date from the second. Further, all four copies in the first group carry the initials of W.G. as indicating authorship, while the five others are anonymous. Destinations are likewise varied: the copies in the first group are all addressed to the young Counts of East Friesland by name, while in the second group only B is so addressed, the name of Christopher being however omitted, as it is also in D. G and J are seemingly intended for 'the Lords and States of the Empire of Germany . . . yet principally the Lord or Earl of Emden', and C is addressed simply to 'my gracious Lord'. E, the remaining copy, should probably be classified in a category of its own. The text is somewhat different from that of the rest, and the numbering of the component 'Articles' discrepant. The handwriting is that of the various contemporary documents of political interest with which it is bound, among which are included George Nedham's 'Articles for reformation of the deceits used in the receiving and paying of the Queen's Majesty's revenues of Custom, Subsidy and Impost'.[137] The whole comprises a thick book formerly known as volume XXI of the Yelverton manuscripts, which seems to have come into existence as a file of reference papers, the property of Robert Beale when he served as Clerk to the Privy Council.[138]

Within the first group of copies, A and D stand out by reason of their size. They are large paper copies, more impressive in their format and more legible in their writing than the others. They may well come from the same pen. The presence of D among the Lansdowne manuscripts indicates that it was once the property of the Lord Treasurer Burghley himself. May it not be that it was written out specially for his benefit? The inference is strengthened by the apologetic sentence inserted into the introduction, to the effect that if the author had been more learned his text might have been made much shorter, and more plain and effectual – in the eyes of George Nedham the Lord Treasurer doubtless appeared not only as his every-busy patron, a mighty personage of political weight, but also as a deft and most learned man. With this attribution as a pointer, it might be suggested that A, the other large paper copy, was intended for Sir Walter Myldmay, also a patron of Nedham, which would explain how it passed into the possession of his descendant the present Earl Fitzwilliam. C, a small paper copy but finely bound in leather, bears every mark of being intended for presentation. It is headed THE EPISTLE, without reference to the Counts of East Friesland, and addressed simply to 'my gracious lord'. It is not impossible that it was meant for the Earl of Leicester, who liked his possessions to be of good quality.[139] The only other fragment of information worth mentioning is that by the early seventeenth century G, H and J were fairly certainly in the library of the first Earl of Bridgwater, and may have been owned by his father, the Lord Chancellor Ellesmere.[140]

A problem, probably insoluble, is posed by the precise dating of the postscript in each surviving copy of the 'Letter' to one or other of the first two days of September 1572. This need not, of course, be taken to signify that all or even any of them was exactly completed on the day mentioned, though it might be supposed that none was written out long after the indicated date. But why 1572, and why September? Two possibly relevant considerations come to mind. In internal English politics, there was the appointment of Burghley as Lord Treasurer in July. Up to a point, he might be counted as a patron of Nedham. Externally, there were the negotiations with the Netherlands government which, with an unquenchable revolt on its hands, was anxious to end the trade embargo of 1569. Discussions were also in progress with a view to the marriage of Queen Elizabeth to a French prince. Was it more than a coincidence that news of the St Bartholomew massacres was beginning to filter into England in August 1572?[141] It provoked a wave of anti-papal sentiment, perhaps strong enough to remind the more militant protestants in London of the existence of the 'Letter'. If the copies were made or started in mid-September or later, the back-dating might be explained as an attempt to substantiate the popular belief that the papal bogey was international, dominating the King of Spain as much as the rulers of France. A topical implication would be that the House of Burgundy on past showing was an ally no more worthy than the House of Valois. But we are on very speculative ground.

An attempt to describe the dissemination of copies of the 'Letter' is severely hampered by reason of the pains taken by Nedham to hide in the shadows. Nowhere is his name attached to any of the texts. And even when writing to his patron Burghley about high matters with a bearing on politics, he had learnt to leave his letters unsigned. This is readily explicable by a glance back at the events of 1564, when George Nedham for a short time held the centre of City limelight, and as a result his mercantile career had been broken.[142] This alone would have sufficed to make him furtive when dealing with matters above his station in life. But in addition, we may well surmise that Burghley, whatever his personal sympathy for Nedham's point of view, had no wish to allow it unrestricted publicity. Not merely were there privy councillors hostile to it, but down to the Anglo-Netherlands breach of 1569 the queen had perforce to look upon Philip II as her closest ally; and for some years subsequently the possibility remained that the traditional Anglo-Burgundian alliance might again be conjured into existence, with some consequent opprobrium for Nedham and his works. Besides, Elizabeth was sensitive to foreign criticism of her sovereignty or government; her envoys in both France and Spain during the 1560s at one time or another had to object to the publication of books reflecting on her office as ruler of England. It would have been difficult to pursue these protests if she were known to be encouraging or merely harbouring an anti-Spanish or anti-Netherlands malcontent. Hence the cloak of secrecy in which Nedham perforce wrapped himself, and hence too his complete neglect of the printing press.

Conversely, there were various reasons for the growth of anti-Spanish sentiment, especially perhaps from *c.* 1569, of which Nedham's 'Letter' supplied no more than one.[143] It is difficult to be sure of his influence save when phrases taken from the 'Letter' or other writings of his are actually cited; but in fact it is possible to mention some instances. For example, among the state papers for 1565 there exist a couple of copies of a summary of his arguments in favour of keeping a mart at Emden, one of them endorsed in the hand of Secretary Cecil.[144] There are palpable echoes of Nedham's language in the pungent state paper of 1572 or thereabouts, headed 'Reasons to move the forbearing of traffic with Flanders'; four copies of this document survive, scattered in various archives, so that in its day it must have passed under numerous pairs of eyes.[145] A striking instance of direct borrowing from the 'Letter' is supplied by Richard Hakluyt's *A Discourse of Western Planting*, a short treatise penned in 1584 at the request of Walter Raleigh. It was the purpose of Hakluyt in this work to point out the disadvantages of relying on the Netherlands as a market for English cloths, and to urge the colonisation of North America by Englishmen to whom 'in short time we shall vent as great a mass of cloth . . . as ever we did in the Netherlands'.[146] He developed this theme by drawing directly upon the 'Letter', which he described as 'a notable discourse', written by 'a man of great observation'.[147] He may well have been aware that the elderly quay-keeper George Nedham was the author, if only through City gossip, but he warily refrained from divulging any dangerous secrets. Much of the information about the pattern of English foreign trade and the political dangers presented by an overweening Spanish monarchy, as he viewed them, was taken from this source.

But the most wholesale borrower from the text of the 'Letter' was John Wheeler, Secretary to the Company of Merchants Adventurers of England, the Fellowship to which George Nedham had once belonged. In 1601, Wheeler printed *A Treatise of Commerce* in defence of the Company, which was then under formidable attack from interloping and other interests both English and foreign.[148] The world of international trade was no longer what it had been in the days of Nedham. The Company had long since left Antwerp, King Philip II was dead, his Netherlands in obstinate revolt against his successor, and English foreign trade had developed direct links with distant markets in the Levant and elsewhere. The general political ideas of Nedham were consequently of small interest to Wheeler. But he found the 'Letter' to be a useful quarry of information, and he embodied large parts of it in his own narrative, without acknowledgment.[149] In particular, he silently appropriated Nedham's description of the commodity trade of the Merchants Adventurers at Antwerp, often word for word. Thus Wheeler's account of English cloth sales at Antwerp, including the figures of sixty thousand white and forty thousand coloured cloths, has been lifted bodily from the 'Letter', as if the passage of nearly forty years had left unchanged the business of the merchants.[150]

The descriptive information originally collected by Nedham thus passed into the general treasury of printed historical knowledge of later centuries through Wheeler's book. A brief reference to some channels along which Nedham's round figures of sixty thousand white and forty thousand coloured cloths were conveyed may serve as illustration. In the mid eighteenth century, they were cited by the annalist John Smith in his anthology *Memoirs of Wool* where he summarised the descriptive portions of Wheeler's *Treatise*, *i.e.* mostly the pages drawn from Nedham's 'Letter'.[151] This indirect resuscitation of the 'Letter' was continued in the twentieth century with the third volume of the much-used collection of *Tudor*

Economic Documents edited by R. H. Tawney and E. Power, published in 1924 and subsequently reprinted. The editors, justifiably enough, here printed a couple of dozen pages drawn from Wheeler's *Treatise*.[152] Among them are included descriptive passages covering the trading activities of the Merchants Adventurers derived partly *verbatim* and part in summary from the 'Letter', so that successive generations of students have perforce read about the sixty thousand white and forty thousand coloured English cloths still being shipped abroad at the end of the reign of Elizabeth, though the figures were originally offered by Nedham and refer to the volume of traffic forty years earlier.[153]

Ultimately in the late nineteenth century the actual text of the 'Letter to the Earls of East Friesland' once more came to light. Like so much else, it was re-discovered by William Cunningham, the pioneering economic historian. The version used by him was B, though he also knew of the existence of E and F.[154] At about the same time, the Belgian scholar Baron J. M. B. C. Kervyn de Lettenhove in his collection of documents bearing on Anglo-Netherlands political relations in the later sixteenth century disclosed his acquaintance with E. He did not print it, perhaps because it was, in his words, *fort étendu*; but he entered a brief note to indicate its importance.[155] B was also used by Richard Ehrenberg in his exploration of the relations of the Free City of Hamburg with England.[156] A generation later, E. C. G. Brunner too became aware of the significance of the 'Letter', and in a footnote to his study of the iconoclastic outbreaks in the Netherlands in 1566 and the simultaneous closure of the Baltic by the King of Denmark, he made known his intention to publish an edition of B; but this does not appear to have been achieved.[157] The text of the 'Letter' is therefore printed here for the first time as a whole.

List of abbreviations used in the notes to the Introduction

Add.	BL, Additional MSS
APC	*Acts of the Privy Council*

BL	London, British Library, Department of Manuscripts
C 66	PRO, Patent Rolls
Cotton	BL, Cotton MSS
CPR	*Calendar of Patent Rolls*
CSPD	*Calendar of State Papers Domestic*
CSPF	*Calendar of State Papers Foreign*
E 122	PRO, Exchequer, Customs Accounts
E 163	PRO, Miscellanea of the Exchequer
Hagedorn, *OH*	B. Hagedorn, *Ostfrieslands Handel und Schiffahrt im 16. Jahrhundert* (Berlin, 1910)
Harl.	BL, Harleian MSS
HMC	*Historical Manuscripts Commission*
KL	J. M. B. C. Baron Kervyn de Lettenhove and L. Gillidts van Severen, *Relations politiques des Pays-Bas et de l'Angleterre sous le règne de Philippe II.* Eleven vols. (Brussels, 1882–1900)
Lansd.	BL, Lansdowne MSS
Pepys Papers	Pepys Papers at Magdalene College, Cambridge
PRO	London, Chancery Lane, Public Record Office
PROB	PRO, Probate Administration Prerogative Court of Canterbury
Royal	BL, Royal MSS
SP 1	PRO, State Papers, Henry VIII
SP 12	PRO, State Papers Domestic, Elizabeth I
SP 46	PRO, State Papers Domestic, Supplementary
SP 70	PRO, State Papers Foreign, Elizabeth I
Smedt	O. de Smedt, *De Engelse Natië te Antwerpen in de 16e eeuw*, two vols. (Antwerp, 1950–4)

Notes to the Introduction

1 G. A. Holmes, 'The "Libel of English Policy" ', *English Historical Review*, LXXVI (1961), 193–216.

2 Even the *Memorandum for the understanding of the Exchange* has now been shown to be the work of Smith, not Gresham – M. Dewar, *Sir Thomas Smith, a Tudor intellectual in office* (London, 1964), 5, 76.
3 A. B. Ferguson, *The articulate citizen and the English renaissance* (Durham, N.C., 1965).
4 'Drei volkswirthschaftliche Denkschriften aus der Zeit Heinrichs VIII von England', ed. R. Pauli, *Abhandlungen der königlichen Gesellschaft der Wissenschaften zu Göttingen* (Göttingen, 1878), 15–77: these have mostly been reprinted in *Tudor Economic Documents*, ed. R. H. Tawney and E. Power (London, 1924), III, 90–129; *A Discourse of the Common Weal*, ed. E. Lamond (Cambridge, 1893): later ed. by M. Dewar (Charlottesville, Virginia, 1969); T. Wilson, *A Discourse upon Usury*, ed. R. H. Tawney (London, 1925); *Memorandum for the understanding of the Exchange*, ed. R. de Roover (Cambridge, Mass., 1949).
5 *Infra*, pp. 34–6.
6 London, Guildhall Library, Register of freemen, MS. 512, m. 12v.
7 He can readily be identified in the pedigree of Needham of Thornsett, at Harl. 1,174, no. 284, f. 158.
8 Register of freemen, *ut supra*.
9 Thus Edmund Nedham, of the Grocers' Company, was shipping cloths abroad at this time – see London customs roll 1553–4, E 122/87/4, entries for 18 and 20 June and 11 September 1554.
10 W. Brulez, 'L'Exportation des Pays-Bas vers l'Italie par voie de terre au milieu du XVIe siècle', *Annales*, XIV (1959), 470.
11 Smedt, II, 376n., 438, 447.
12 Typescript list of the members of the Mercers' Company at Mercers' Hall.
13 Smedt, II, 304, 480–1, 582–3.
14 Nedham to Burghley, undated *c.* 1574, Lansd. 18/67. This letter, characteristically unsigned, is endorsed with the name of Nedham by Burghley's secretary Hicks.
15 E 122/87/4.
16 £40 for a pack of ten cloths would have been cheap.
17 E 122/86/7, m. 26.
18 G. D. Ramsay, 'The Recruitment and Fortunes of some London Freemen in mid-sixteenth century', *Economic History Review*, sec. ser., XXXI (1978), pp. 526–40.
19 This seems to be the only mention of his name in the volume of Acts of Court of the Mercers' Company 1560–93 at Mercers' Hall.
20 See the 'Articles', Add. 35, 207, ff. 12 *et seq.*
21 *Short Title Catalogue*, (repr. 1950) no. 10,024.
22 Brulez, 'L'Exportation des Pays-Bas vers l'Italie' *ut supra*, 485.
23 *Infra*, 134.
24 Add. 35,207, f. 6v. The reference is to the hold-up of January–March 1545, well documented in the State Papers, SP 1.
25 The episode is described in G. D. Ramsay, *The City of London in International Politics* (Manchester, 1975), 120–5.

26 Add. 35,207, ff. 12–13.
27 *Ib.*, f. 8.
28 It is now Add. 35,207.
29 'Book', f. 2.
30 *Ib.*, f. 2.
31 *Ib.*, f. 6.
32 *Ib.*, f. 9.
33 *Ib.*, f. 8.
34 *Ib.*, f. 10.
35 How long the drafting of the 'Book' occupied Nedham can only be guessed. It was begun after the events in Scotland in 1560, to which reference was made at f. 3v; a further reference at f. 9 to the thirteenth year of Henry VII, *i.e.* August 1497–8, as 64 years past suggests 1561–2 as the moment of composition. It might well have been 1563 by the time the splendidly-produced copy now at Add. 35,207 reached the queen.
36 *CPR 1560–3*, 462. Perhaps it was at this time that he also acquired some property in Canterbury, of which he disposed in 1583, C 66/1233, m. 40.
37 M. B. Donald, *Elizabethan Copper* (London, 1955), 18, 72–7 etc.
38 The events summarised in this paragraph are treated more fully by G. D. Ramsay, *op. cit.*, 179 *et seq.*
39 Clough to Gresham, undated early 1564, Cotton, Galba B xi, no. 67.
40 Nedham to Cecil, 13 April 1564, SP 70/70/256.
41 Harl. 287, no. 3, f. 4.
42 Nedham fully appreciated the dependence of the industrial population upon the regular delivery of English cloths – *infra*, arts. 45 and 46.
43 Silva to Regent, 1 April 1566, KL, IV, 276.
44 *Infra*, 53.
45 Hagedorn, *OH*, 186. The gracious letter from the queen to the Countess Anna and her three sons, dated 10 February, is at Royal, 13 B 1, f. 125v.
46 Nedham's work for the copper-mining venture is treated by Donald, *Elizabethan Copper*, 72–7 etc.
47 List of shareholders in *ib.*, 242.
48 Anon. (Nedham) to Burghley, 24 April 1572, KL, VI, 396–8.
49 Anon. (Nedham) to Leicester, undated *c.* 1568, Pepys Papers, II. p. 613.
50 Nedham to Burghley, undated *c.* 1574, Lansd. 18/67. The grant was not entered on the patent roll, doubtless because it lay in the gift of the Lord Treasurer and not the Crown.
51 *Ib.*
52 H. A. Lloyd, 'Camden, Carmarden and the Customs', *English Historical Review*, LXXXV (1970), 776–87.
53 Hochstetter *et al.* to Cecil, 20 Sept. 1565, SP 12/37/43, cited Donald, *op. cit.*, 72–3.
54 Winchester to Mildmay, 7 May 1567, SP 46/28, f. 60.
55 There is some account of Pickering in the *Dictionary of National Bio-*

graphy. Nedham's letter is in the Pepys Papers, II, p. 613. There is a summary at *HMC Pepys*, 180. The rest of the paragraph derives from this letter.

56 Merchants Adventurers to Privy Council, undated *c*. 1578, SP 12/127/88.

57 Roger Edward to Cecil, 29 Mar. 1569, SP 12/49/75.

58 *Ib*. to Marsh, 28 May 1569, SP 12/49/88; anon. (Nedham) to Burghley, 24 April 1572, KL, VI, 396–8.

59 *Ib*.

60 *Ib*.

61 Anon. (Nedham) to Burghley, undated *c*. 1575, Lansd. 26/45. There can be no reasonable doubt as to the authorship of this unsigned letter, from internal evidence alone.

62 *Infra*, 33 et seq.

63 Nedham to Cecil, *c*. May 1572, Lansd. 110/39. This letter is unsigned but endorsed 'Nedham Customs' in the hand of Burghley.

64 1 Eliz., *c*. 11. See discussion by B. Dietz, *The Port and Trade of Early Elizabethan London*, Documents (London Record Society, VIII, 1972), introduction, *passim*.

65 Anon. (prob. G. Nedham), Articles for reformation, undated *c*. 1573, Add. 48,020, ff. 215–16.

66 This paragraph is based on *ib*., ff. 215–23 *passim*.

67 Nedham to Cecil, *c*. May 1572, Lansd. 110/39.

68 *Ib*. to *Ib*., undated *c*. 1574, Lansd. 18/67.

69 Zweveghem and Boisschot to Requesens, 15 Mar. 1574, KL, VII, 73–8.

70 Burghley to Myldmay, 16 Dec. 1577, SP 46/31, f. 124.

71 For the terms, see list of quays at Lansd. 35/38.

72 Report of Osborne and Fanshawe, 11 April 1579, E 163/14/4.

73 The struggle, not relevant for present purposes, is comparatively well documented. A further official decision, again in favour of Nedham, is recorded at Lansd. 31/30.

74 Letters of administration were issued to Francis Nedham, PROB 6/3, f. 119.

75 Conyers Read, *Mr. Secretary Walsingham and the Policy of Queen Elizabeth* (Oxford, 1925), II, 421, III, 246. Francis Nedham was made free of the Mercers' Company by patrimony in 1589 – entry in typescript List of Members, Mercers' Hall.

76 Customs officers to Burghley, 15 June 1596, SP 12/259/15.

77 His will is at PROB 11/101/30.

78 J. Foster, *Alumni Oxonienses*, III (Oxford, 1891), 1055.

79 Information about the career of Gnapheus is to be found in the edition of his poem published by H. Babucke, *Wilhelm Gnapheus, ein Lehrer aus dem Reformationszeitalter* (Emden, 1875).

80 Babucke, *op. cit*., 15.

81 The answer of the Merchants Adventurers to the Countess Anna, 13 Nov. 1562, is at Royal, 13 B 1, ff. 84–5.

82 'Book', f. 8v.

83 Anything like a precise date is impossible to determine. *Vide supra*, n. 35.
84 Merchants Adventurers to Countess Anna etc., 18 Jan. 1564, Royal, 13 B 1, f. 103v.
85 Hagedorn, *OH*, 173.
86 Nedham to Cecil, 13 April 1564, SP 70/70/256.
87 Hagedorn, *op. cit.*, 175.
88 *Infra*, art. 63.
89 *Ib.*, art. 64.
90 'Book', f. 2.
91 *Infra*, preface and arts. 1, 2, 3, 33, 35, 36, 70, 71.
92 Pr. KL, IV, 144–6.
93 *Supra*, 12.
94 Evidence that the 'Letter' was now shown to Cecil is in the unsigned letter of Nedham to Cecil, 24 April 1572, SP 70/123/67, pr. KL, VI, 396–8: 'I made a booke of a large dyscours and showed the same to Yowr Honnor'.
95 *Infra*, art. 39. Cf. Ramsay, *City of London*, 26.
96 *Infra*, 54.
97 Silva to Regent, 1 April 1566, KL, IV, 276.
98 Cf. *supra*, 1.
99 J. Carion, *The thre bokes of Cronicles, whyche John Carion gathered*, tr. W. Lynne (London, 1550); J. Sleidan, *A famouse cronicle of our time, called Sleidanes commentaries, concerning the state of religion and common wealth, during the raigne of the emperoure Charles the fift*, tr. I. Daus (London, 1560).
100 *Infra*, art. 62.
101 P. Jeannin, *Les marchands au XVIe siècle* (Paris, 1957), 139.
102 *Infra*, art. 32, p. 83.
103 *Ib.*, art. 1 p. 55. He had used much the same language in the 'Book' – *supra*, 8.
104 *Infra*, art. 34, p. 86.
105 *Ib.*, art. 32, p. 84. See the more detailed approach to this topic by J. Craeybeckx, *Algemene Geschiedenis der Nederlanden*, IV (Utrecht, 1952), 114–19.
106 *Infra*, art. 32.
107 *Ib.*, art. 13.
108 *Ib.*, art 16.
109 The importance of the English at Antwerp has been analysed by W. Brulez, 'Le commerce international des Pays-Bas au XVIe siècle: essai d'appréciation quantitative', *Revue belge de Philologie et d'Histoire*, XLVI (1968), 1205–21. English version in *Acta Historica Neerlandica*, IV (1970), 20–48.
110 *Infra*, art. 2.
111 G. Asaert, *De Antwerpse scheepvaart in de XVe eeuw (1394–1480). Bijdrage tot de ekonomische geschiedenis van de stad Antwerpen* (Brussels, 1973), 404.
112 *Infra*, art. 3.
113 Smedt, I, 84. For the rise of Antwerp, see R. Doehaerd, *Etudes anver-*

soises (Paris, 1963), I, esp. 26–66; H. van der Wee, *The Growth of the Antwerp Market and the European Economy (fourteenth–sixteenth centuries)* (The Hague, 1963), II, 7–207. There is a useful summary by R. Davis, 'The Rise of Antwerp and its English Connection, 1406–1510', *Trade, Government and Economy in Pre-Industrial England*, ed. D. C. Coleman and A. H. John (London, 1976), 2–20.

114 L. Guicciardini, *Descrittione di tutti i Paesi Bassi* (Antwerp, 1567).

115 *Infra*, art. 11.

116 *Infra*, art. 12.

117 *Infra*, arts. 41 to 45.

118 These numbers have been reached by drawing upon the figures printed by J. D. Gould, *The Great Debasement* (Oxford, 1970), 181, and incorporating supplementary information from E 163/13/2. A ninth has then been added to the resultant totals to allow for the duty-free 'wrapper' cloth, which at London and most other ports was one in ten. At certain other ports, including Hull, it was more generous.

119 *Infra*, art. 42. The *écu* was valued at 4*s*. 2½*d*. *c*. 1558 – list of 'Staple money' quotations, Cotton Galba C II, f. 252/254v. It has been shown by B. Dietz, 'Antwerp and London: the structure and balance of trade in the 1560's', *Wealth and Power in Tudor England*, ed. E. W. Ives, R. J. Knecht and J. J. Scarisbrick (London, 1978), 190, that in the summer months of 1565 not quite two-thirds of the cloths shipped, by English and Hanse merchants, from London were being dispatched to Antwerp. The proportion rises to rather more than two-thirds if only shipments by English merchants are taken into account. However it might be rash to assume that trade during this season and year was representative of activities during the whole decade.

120 Smedt, II, 356 *et seq*.

121 *Infra*, art. 46.

122 *Infra*, art. 45.

123 *Infra*, art. 46.

124 *Infra*, art. 57.

125 *Infra*, art. 58.

126 *Infra*, art. 59.

127 *Infra*, art. 56.

128 H. Schilling, *Niederländische Exulanten im 16. Jahrhundert* (Gütersloh, 1972), 65–9 etc.; B. Hagedorn, *Ostfrieslands Handel und Schiffahrt vom Ausgang des 16. Jahrhunderts* (Berlin, 1912), 266 *et seq*. See also the recent discussion by H. Schilling, 'Reformation und Burgerfreiheit. Emdens Weg zur calvinistischen Stadtrepublik', in *Stadt und Kirche im 16. Jahrhundert*, ed. B. Moeller, *Schriften des Vereins für Reformationsgeschichte*, 190 (Gütersloh, 1978), 128–61.

129 *Supra*, 12.

130 *Supra*, 13.

131 *Infra*, 57.

132 *Infra*, arts. 17, 18, 37, 38, 39, 40, 41, 52, 53, 54, 66.

133 Edward to Marsh, 28 May 1569, SP 12/49/88. This document has been incorrectly listed in *CSPF 1572–4*, 92, no. 293.

134 Anon. (Nedham) to Burghley, 24 April 1572, SP 70/123/67, pr. KL, VI, 396–8.
135 *Ib.* to *ib.*, undated *c.* 1575, Lansd. 26/45. Nedham here somewhat loosely implies that it was the Latin translation that was sent to the Counts, but he also states that he has it himself. On this document see above p. 44, note 61.
136 *Ib.*
137 At ff. 215 *et seq.*
138 On the Yelverton manuscripts, see *HMC Second Report, Calthorpe*, 39–46.
139 Other distinctions between the copies might be mentioned. Thus the component sections are headed 'Cap.', not 'Art.' in D, and the headings are omitted altogether in B and E. There are considerable variations in the bindings, the quality of the paper used, and even in the wording of the text. But further pursuit of these points hardly seems to offer profit.
140 Evidence of library marks, kindly supplied by Miss Mary L. Robertson, of the Huntington Library.
141 Conyers Read, *Lord Burghley and Queen Elizabeth* (London, 1960), 86–7. See also *infra*, 134–5.
142 *Supra*, 13.
143 The general topic has been competently surveyed by W. S. Maltby, 'The Black Legend in England, 1558–1660', unpublished thesis, Duke University, 1967.
144 SP 12/36/4 and 5.
145 PRO copy at SP 15/20/64; two in BL at Cotton Calig. B V, no. 56, and Add. 48,020, ff. 360 *et seq.*; and one in Northants Records Office at MS. W. (A) 6, vii, 3 (endorsed with the name of Thomas Aldersey). There is also the briefer summary, 'Notes out of the exhortation to the Princes of Germany' in the PRO at SP 70/147/243. Echoes of Nedham's language may be detected also at SP 12/41/57, doubtfully calendared as *c.* 1566.
146 Text edited by E. G. R. Taylor in *The Original Writings and Correspondence of the two Richard Hakluyts*, Hakluyt Society, second series, LXXVII (1935), 211–326. Like the 'Letter', and doubtless for much the same reasons, it was not printed at the time.
147 *Original Writings, ut supra*, 237.
148 There were editions, more or less identical, at both London and Middelburg; G. B. Hotchkiss has edited a modern issue. (New York, 1931).
149 Thus his account of Anglo-Netherlands relations at 28–31 is largely taken from arts. 72–8 *infra*, and of the origins of Antwerp prosperity at 15–17 from arts 3 and 4.
150 Wheeler, *Treatise*, 21–2 from arts. 41–2.
151 J. Smith, *Chronicon Rusticum-Commerciale; or, Memoirs of Wool &c.* (London, 1747), I, 116–21.
152 *Tudor Economic Documents*, III, 280–304.
153 *Ib.*, 283.

154 W. Cunningham, *The Growth of English Industry and Commerce in Modern Times*, fourth ed. (Cambridge, 1907), I, 74 n. 3, 224–6. First published in 1882.
155 KL, III (1883), 664, no. MCCLXII.
156 R. Ehrenberg, *Hamburg und England im Zeitalter der Königin Elisabeth* (Jena, 1896), 70 n. 25.
157 E. C. G. Brunner, 'Die dänische Verkehrsperre und der Bildersturm in den Niederländen im Jahre 1566', *Hansische Geschichtsblätter*, XXXIII (1928), 103n.

A letter to the Earls of East Friesland

To the right noble, honourable, and my gracious lords, the Lord Edzard, the Lord John, and the Lord Christopher, the Lords and Earls of East Friesland, W.G. wisheth the Grace of God and health unto you all, that in all Honours you may reign over us.

When I call to remembrance, most gracious lords, the great alterations and changes of the imperial state, and the dangerous government of the same, and into what peril of late years our imperial princes of Germany have brought themselves and their posterity by suffering so many large and fair countries, strong cities, towns, valiant soldiers and rich merchants that were lately imperial to be taken from them and their governments and joined to the House of Burgundy, which Burgundians by their policy and colourable dealings do by little and little shake, weaken and rend away the strength, authority and government of the Empire, it makes men, and many more that be of great knowledge and judgment rather firmly believe than doubt (considering of what power and strength King Philip is of himself besides such aid as he may have from his friends in Italy and Germany that be of the Popish religion) that in short time, if it be not foreseen, he will bring the whole Empire under the government of Spain and the House of Burgundy. Which thing is well known to all men [that] his father the Emperor Charles many years most earnestly sought and desired. And to this day too, the same is practised by the Spanish and Burgundish Council, as by their proceedings it doth manifestly appear and may justly be proved.

And therefore it standeth your Graces upon, with the aid and help of the imperial princes to join yourselves together and to withstand these attempts, and not suffer the Burgundish as it were thus sleepingly to creep in and spoil the Empire, into which by colourable means they be so far entered; especially, having the town of Groningen so much at their commandment that they lack nothing to bring their crafty doings and purpose to effect, but only the getting of your Graces' country of East Friesland and the river of Ems into their hands. And what policies have been used and attempts made to get the same! First, from your Graces' father; and then from my most gracious Lady your mother, she being a widow; and now in your time from you, your Graces know best. Which country of yours of East Friesland and the river of Ems be now the only key, assurance and strength of the whole Empire to and from the seas: which if your Graces and other imperial princes did know as well as I and some other do, I mean that in the safe keeping or losing of the said country and river the liberty or bondage of the whole Empire doth consist, it would give you and them both just cause, if ye have any love to yourselves, regard to your honours or care for your country and posterity, to look to this matter in time, and take example what the Spanish government is by your neighbours of the *stift* of Utrecht, the county of Gelderland and the town of Groningen and other places that were late imperial, lest (under your Graces' corrections) by careless and ignorant government, in overmuch trusting to your security, yourselves, your country and liberty may be overthrown before you think there is any danger or hurt meant towards you.

And therefore I do beseech your Graces that other princes, your neighbours and friends, may be made privy to this that I write, wherein I have set forth into what peril they be now brought. Whereof I know many of them be utterly ignorant, not only of what importance the safe keeping of your Graces' country of East Friesland and the river of Ems is to them and the whole Empire, but also of the great dangers wherin you and they be wrapped at this present; neither know they any means how to remedy the same unless it were by plain force or making open war against King Philip, which if it should happen (as God defend) would set great trouble and breed many factions amongst the princes of Germany; and yet doubtful would it be, what would be the end considering (as I have said) of what great strength King Philip and his Popish friends be. Therefore considering how well the time serveth, according to my bounden duty, as a lover of my native country I have showed my opinion how you princes may with quietness not only withstand and redress all these perils, dangers and practices that our imperial state and princes be wrapped in, and avoid the uncertain hazards and charges that might follow, if the same should be redressed by war; but also how you may with quietness take away from King Philip and bring into the country of East Friesland and other towns of Germany the great treasure and force which hath made him and his ancestors and their subjects of the Netherlands of such power and wealth as they be grown unto: such wealth, I meant, as wherewith his father the Emperor Charles hath been, and in the end King Philip will be, the troubler of all the princes and kings in Europe.

All these matters, I say, may yet be easily redressed now, if your Graces and other our imperial princes will but join together and maintain the ancient liberties, freedoms and customs of the Empire, and suffer no new tolls or exactions to be raised. And withal, if you will embrace and enter in league and friendship with the English prince and the merchants her subjects that, as it were by God's providence, of their own good will be now freely come to you, both with their persons and also their ships and goods, to traffic in your town of Emden and country of East Friesland and other towns of the Empire, upon your only word and promise of honour, without any demand of such assurance for them and their goods as they might have had if they would have gone to divers other places, besides large sums of money given them freely.

So that, in truth, your Graces and other princes, towns and merchants both in Germany and Eastland, if you and they consider the matter well, have great cause to be glad and thank God for it, that they are so happily arrived hither. For we may take example by King Philip's Netherlands of Brabant, Flanders, Holland, Zealand, Artois, Hainault, into what state and wealth those barren countries and towns be grown in few years by the amity and friendship of the English princes and their merchants, by whose traffic and commodities comes such incredible profits and benefits many and sundry ways as no man will think or believe, neither myself could have believed unless I had searched and made just proof and trial thereof, as shall appear hereafter in this book, which I have set forth to the intent that both your Graces and all other imperial princes, rulers, merchants and other people may plainly see and understand that the amity and friendship of the English prince hath been the original and the only cause of all that great glory, fame and wealth that the House of Burgundy hath gotten: with which riches, as I have said, they have enlarged their dominions of Burgundy and Spain, the doing wherof hath set such dissension amongst Christian princes in Europe that it hath been the only cause that the Turk is entered so far both into Hungary and also other places of Christendom.

And therefore, seeing it hath pleased Almighty God to send into your Graces' country that prince's subjects with their commodities, whereby such wealth and strength may be taken from your enemies and brought into your town of Emden and country of East Friesland (being an ancient and principal member of the Empire) by reason of that notable river of Ems; whose goodness for lack of traffic fame hath not published and made known to the world till now to be such as it is; nor yet to stand so commodiously for the course of all the merchants of the world to resort to and from by sea and land, as well as it doth to Antwerp; and forasmuch as it is not yet openly known how [in] sundry ways God hath blessed your country with such excellent gifts of nature as Man cannot take from it; and that to this our time, God hath kept the same obscure and unknown, yea almost unknown to your next neighbours; and that it pleased him now by his divine providence to make the same your country, and his blessings given to it to be a public and known place to all nations, that it stands as commodiously and as safe as Antwerp itself, and that the passage unto it to resort to and fro by sea or by land is as easy: you are to think it a sure sign of his great grace and goodness towards you and all the state of Germany, and that his pleasure is to enlarge and set out further his praise and glory, and that by these his motions he means to show you the way how you shall restore the torn, weak, decayed and variable government of our Empire into his former beauty, strength and nobleness. And that through your doings a good, sure and quiet peace might be had through all Christendom, both for religion and other quarrels and discords amongst all Christian princes. And the better to encourage you forward, he doth by these his motions show you how to take your enemy's sword out of his hands and put it into your own, as hereafter in this book shall be declared; which things doth give your Graces and other princes great cause to be thankful, and not to let pass these good motions of God but to take time, while time serveth. And specially to embrace and seek the amity of that prince and to cherish and maintain her merchants and all other that will come to traffic with you.

And for the better accomplishing hereof, it behoveth all you imperial princes lovingly and friendly to join together in one, and to consult with one another about it; and with as much care, diligence and policy as may be, to seek to maintain our old imperial laws, customs, liberties and freedoms, that all merchants may have a quiet and safe passage to and from with their persons and goods throughout the Empire. For King Philip this last year *anno* 1564 being afraid that that profitable nation and their commodities would depart [from] his country and leave it and come to your Graces' city of Emden, sought not only by his unlawful proclamations and commandments to break and violate the old liberties, freedoms and customs of the Empire; but also to discourage the said English merchants the more, by his friends he laboured the merchants of Germany and Eastland, and by his own authority commanded the merchants of Italy and Spain, that they should not come to traffic at Emden. The sufferance of this, I say, was not only a foul dishonour, but the example as perilous to encourage both him and other princes to do the like or worse against you, seeing you be so careless and suffer so quietly such great wrongs to be laid upon you, as though you imperial princes either cared not, one to see another country spoiled; or, seeing your neighbour's house afire, ye took no care for your own.

Therefore I say unto you, most gracious lords, it standeth you upon to look well unto this matter, and with good advice and counsel to make others [the] princes your neighbours privy not only of the great danger that both there you stand in, but also with all diligence to embrace and follow this good offer and blessing of God; and specially not to suffer this little member, your country East Friesland, to be molested nor troubled by the House of Burgundy, nor cut off from the body of the Empire. For if it should so happen, ere it were long the highest prince to the poorest ploughman in Germany should feel the smart, as shall be declared hereafter in this book. Which I have rudely set forth (as I said) to the end that your Graces and all other imperial princes and their people may know into what peril they be brought, and how the same may be remedied by the amity of the English prince and the traffic of her merchants. Who, being brought into such a league and amity with you and other imperial princes as they have been with the House of Burgundy, will be found and proved so necessary and profitable to the whole imperial state and subjects, considering how the Empire stands at this present time, that assuredly I think no one nation or state in Europe in all respects may be so profitable to us for our assurance, strength and quietness. As hereafter I will prove to your Graces by sundry true examples, wherof many be in memory of men yet living, that can witness how towns and countries did prosper where English merchants did traffic and abide, and how the said towns and countries have decayed straight from whence they have departed.

Which proofs I shall, according to they I have seen, read and known, justly and truly set out, desiring your Graces to take this my simple collection in good part. And although my phrase be but rude and my style but tedious, for lack of that skill that a man meanly learned might easily mend; yet I trust your Graces will bear with my barren wit and accept well of that mind that meaneth your Graces and my country and all other imperial princes and their people as much good as behoveth a faithful and careful subject to have in his heart.

[MS. Lansdowne 205 has after 'tedious,': and by the learned might have been made much shorter, and more plaine and effectual, I most humbly beseech your Graces . . .]

Art. 1

It is openly known to all people, my gracious Lords, that have travelled and seen the Base Countries of King Philip named the Netherlands or Base Germany – as Brabant, Flanders, Zealand, Holland, Artois, Hainault – that of themselves they be barren, and in manner bring forth no natural commodities that should draw so great a traffic and resort of merchants unto them as they do, nor get such great wealth as they have: no, they be not able to get in their countries so much corn as will suffice them bread and drink, but are fain to make the most part of their provisions from other foreign countries, their neighbours, for the same. And yet, the said countries do abound most plentifully not only with corn and all other kinds of merchandise from all places of the world; but by the great riches that they have gotten and daily do get, by resort of merchants out of all foreign nations and countries, they have built and do build and maintain great number of strong and fair cities, which are become very populous and full of rich merchants. Besides, in all sorts of most expert and cunning artificers they exceed, that no one country or port in Europe in my opinion may be compared unto them, as I think your Graces hath heard and doth understand.

All this wealth and knowledge they have gotten since the days of the third Edward, by name King of England, which is about two hundred years past, but specially within this hundred and twenty years. For the aforesaid King Edward III about two hundred years ago won the stronghold of Calais from the French nation, which bordered and joined upon the frontier of Flanders at Gravelines:[1] the Earls of Flanders at that time not being under the Duke of Burgundy, but rather vassals or homagers to the French King. The said Earls of Flanders, after the getting of the said town of Calais, for the better assurance and safety of themselves and their country, sought to enter into amity and love with the Kings of England, and so laboured and travailed with the Kings of England (as the old records do show it) to have their merchants resort and haunt their country of Flanders with the merchandises and

[1] Calais fell to the English in 1347.

commodities of England that at length it was granted, and the Kings of England and they concluded in league together.

But to the sequel, what followed on it in short time with little proof: the Flemish prince and people found such profit and commodity by the haunt of the English nation, that to encourage them to continue still and traffic in their country the Earls of Flanders gave and granted to the merchants of England so large and ample privileges and freedoms, which are yet to be showed, that no nation in Europe had the like at that time. By reason of which privileges and freedoms granted, and that the adventure by sea and land into the coasts of Flanders was withal so short and commodious, and in manner without danger to the English merchants, they settled themselves in a town of Flanders named Bruges, and stapled[2] their commodities of England there. And this thing once known and blown abroad, in short time all the merchants of Europe resorted thither and made their habitation there; as, to this very day, their houses yet stand and bear the names of the country or towns of whence the strange merchants were. Thus was Bruges and all the towns of Flanders in few years brought to such wealth and riches, but especially Bruges, that the fame therof was blown almost to the four corners of the world, both for the beautiful buildings and wealth wherein it flowed, and for the concourse of all sorts of merchants that daily resorted thither; the beauty wherof to this day remaineth yet, though the riches and concourse of merchants be altogether failed.

But by reason the Flemish merchants were grown to such wealth, pride and fulness of bread that they did forget and unthankfully deal not only with them alone, by whom their wealth grew: but also their bounden duty to their sovereign Lord and prince, and other their neighbours also, in such sort as they grew to a proud disdain and contempt of all merchants of all strange nations, even of the English merchants too, by whom they received their greatest good and profit. Upon great unsufferable injuries done to them by the Flemings, the

[2] Established a market for.

said English merchants, I say, departed [from] their town and country; from which time of their departure, it is well known that the said country, and specially the town of Bruges, hath grown to great decay and the merchants therof are worn out clean. But, by that way feeling themselves thus scourged and plagued by themselves and their follies, and sorrowing their oversight now full sore, they have many times since made many means and suits to have the traffic of the English merchants again. And now of late, to see their follies the more, they that could not make much of their friends while they had them, have proffered £100,000 unto the said English merchants, with other large proffers of greater and more ample privileges and freedoms then ever they had there before or in any place else. Yea, to say more, they have in manner proffered them a blank paper to tie them to what they list, and to ask what they would, at their pleasure to have the said English merchants to traffic thither again. But the English merchants departed from Bruges to Zealand to a town named Middelburg, whither all other nations followed them straight. But this city of Middelburg stood so near unto the sea that the ditches and marshes of the same, being full of salt and filthy ooze for lack of a fresh river to scour the channel and ditches, bred such a stench and evil air that the merchants that were used to the sweet and wholesome airs in England being in that waterish and moist country were infected with grievous agues and other sickness; so that for their healths' sake they were forced to leave that town. At which time Antwerp, being then a poor simple town standing in Brabant, made a great suit to the English merchants to have them come to them, the which upon the large grants and gifts of privileges and freedoms they made, the said English merchants granted and went unto them. Whose coming was so joyful to the said town of Antwerp, that the rulers and burgesses received them with solemn processions. In which town of Antwerp and in a town named Barrow,[3] about four German miles from Antwerp, the English merchants have remained, with their commodities, to this day.

[3] Bergen-op-Zoom.

Art. 2

Now, to declare somewhat of the state of Antwerp when the English nation first came thither: your Graces shall understand, it was no town of merchants but a town of artificers and of such as lived upon their rents and lands, and of such poor people that lived, as it were, of very husbandry, keeping cattle for milk, butter and cheese, as one part of their town beareth the name therof to this very day. The most part of their houses were covered with straw, and within their walls there were great waste grounds both of meadow and pasture. And to the said town at that time belonged not above six ships, and they were only for their river and never went to the seas; and at this day, there is above a hundred sail of good ships of all sorts belonging to that town. So naked was Antwerp at the first coming of the English merchants which was about the year of our Lord 1494 or therabouts, which is about seventy years past; and yet in the memory of men now living, being able to witness as much as I have written. Thus I have showed your Graces briefly the first coming of the English merchants in Flanders, and how their being there prospered that country and towns, and how by their departure the said country of Flanders and the said town of Bruges decayed; and in like manner I have declared and will declare in what state Antwerp was when the English merchants came thither first; wherin your Graces shall see incredible matters.

Art. 3

I have heard old men say, that be yet living, that at the first coming of the English nation there was not in all Antwerp above four merchants; and they were not adventurers to the seas themselves, but occupied at home in their own town and the countries therabouts. And the townsmen or burgesses, being then but poor and neither able nor skilful to use the trade of merchandise, let out all the best of their houses to strange merchants – as their chambers furnished with beds – and were themselves as servants to the merchants strangers. And their nether rooms of their houses they let out for packhouses, and lodged themselves in cellars and other small corners for profit sake. But within few years the resort of strange nations was so much to that town that houseroom failed and waxed scant; then rents of houses were raised and waxed dear; tolls, excises and all other duties both to the prince and his subjects were wonderfully increased, and the Antwerpians began to wax marvellous rich, so that some fell to use the trade of merchandise and others employed their substance into building. Then old rotten houses covered with straw were pulled down, their void ground built [upon], and many goodly streets and new houses made.

Thus prospered not only the merchants of Antwerp, but all other merchants and towns in Zealand and Holland and all other places in the Base Countries therabout; and also their lands, tenements and houses in the country waxed dear, and the husbandmen rich by the great abundance they breed of all kind of victuals, which were spent by resort of the merchants and shippers by sea and by land. By this intercourse and traffic, all kinds of people were set a-work and gained. But above all the rest, Antwerp from time to time hath waxed better and better, and specially since the beginning and reign of the last Emperor, Charles. [So] that now at this day, the said town of Antwerp is grown to such wealth, strength and beauty as never town was in so short a time since the knowledge of man. And no marvel: for a house that fifty years past was worth forty thalers is worth now at this time £75, which maketh 300 thalers; and a house that was let for 60 thalers is worth at this present £100, which maketh 400 thalers; so that of some houses in that town there is made yearly six or seven hundred thalers rent.[4] Thus is their costly building of house and making of havens, that ships may come within their town, and the building of other things for the commodity of merchants a marvellous thing, and almost incredible to them that have not seen it; besides the fortifying of their town, which fortification is such that the charges therof would trouble the best and richest prince in Europe.

And thus you see, the Netherlands of King Philip are made rich only by the resort of strange merchants. I speak it with

[4] The thaler was a German silver coin, originally from metal mined at Joachimsthal in Bohemia. Also called dollar, as *infra*, 65.

reverence and under your Graces' good correction, for I am lothe to displease with any comparison that is not fitting. But, trust me, the town of Antwerp may be very well likened to a poor young man that setteth up a tennis court, a victualling or a dicing house, who to get guests and customers at the first is diligent to receive, serve and please all sorts of people; for the more resort he hath to his house, the more profit is his. For whosoever it be that loseth, the box ever wins; and howsoever it fares with the guests, the host ever thrives. And so the beggarly host soon riseth rich and licketh the fat from the lips of his guests; and at the length waxeth insolent and proud with the smear of his ill-gotten wealth; and laugheth them to scorn that have greased him most, and careth not for them when he hath a great fleece of the wool, and made them poor and lean. Even so fared it with the merchants of Bruges, and even so fareth it now with the merchants of Antwerp and the Netherlands, who be so greatly increased in riches and knowledge by sea and by land that they have almost eaten out and gotten the whole traffic of all strange nations into their hands, except the merchants of England, as hereafter I will declare. With which merchants of England they begin now to quarrel sundry ways, against all reason and equity, which in time will be (trust well unto it!) the undoing of that town and country as it hath been already of Bruges.

Art. 4

Now I will show your Graces how many strange nations and merchants the Netherlands, and specially the merchants of the town of Antwerp, have eaten out of their trade and occupying. And first I will begin with your German or Dutch merchants. It is not above forty or fifty years past or thereupon, that the merchants of Germany had not only the whole trade in their hands, of all the English cloths and other commodities that served for the merchants in Germany; but also all other commodities that came out of other foreign countries to Antwerp that were meet or served for Germany; and they only bought it up all and carried it to the towns and marts in their country, wherby the merchants of Germany got their greatest wealth. And who hath that trade now in carrying the said commodities into Germany? The merchants of Antwerp. And the Dutch or German merchants in manner do nothing: but in all marts and fairs in Germany the Antwerpians bear the swing, and all such gain as the German merchants were wont to have by that trade of their own country, the Antwerpians and the Netherlands have gotten now. And all remaineth in the hands of the subjects of King Philip, which be wonderfully enriched thereby. So that all that, which was wont to be in the hands of the imperial merchants and subjects, is now taken away, to the enrichment of the Burgundians and their country and to the impoverishment of the imperial country and subjects. And so like to be, more and more, so long as the marts be kept at Antwerp.

Art. 5

Now let us go to the merchants of Eastland, wherein I do comprehend Danzig and those parts, and see how they have sped. Where are the notable merchants of Eastland, I mean of the LXXII privileged towns and cities otherwise called the Hanse Towns, with their great navies of ships which were wont to set a-work and maintain thousands of people? Alas, hath not Amsterdam and other new upstart towns in Holland and Zealand, with their great number of hulks, almost eaten out both the merchants from their trades and the ships and shippers from the seas? For very few there are left at this day, in comparison of them that were twenty or thirty years ago; and the Easterly towns and merchants cannot beware, but they will have a house in Antwerp, and staple their commodities there, where in short time both the rest of the merchants and shippers will be consumed and eaten out clean, if they follow that they have begun. Well, who doth and shall smart for his great decay? The imperial state, that is not only weakened thereby in the loss of their merchants and goods, but also weakened as much by the sea. Who is profited thereby? King Philip and his vassals and subjects both by sea and land, the danger whereof shall be declared hereafter.

Art. 6

Where is the profitable intercourse and trade become that the

Italians, the Germans and the English merchants and others had into Italy, as to Ancona, to Chios, to Venice, Florence, to Rome and other places of Italy, with kerseys,[5] cloths and other English commodities, and other foreign commodities that came out of other countries, that served for Italy? Who be the greatest doers now in Alexandria, Cyprus, Tripoli in Syria and other places of the world, almost beyond the sun? Who serveth Italy now of linen cloth, worsteds, says, tapestry and other such commodities made in the Netherlands? Surely the merchants of Antwerp more than any other nation. Who is impoverished thereby? Germany and the German merchants, England and the English merchants, the Pope and his Italians, and all the merchants of Italy, Venice and the Venetians, and divers others. And who is enriched and strengthened thereby? King Philip, his Netherlands, and subjects.

Art. 7

Now let us go to the good simple Portuguese, who full hungerly for spices almost sails yearly in compass about three quarters of the world; and when he hath brought his spices home, be not the great rich purses of Antwerp, the subjects of King Philip, ready to engross it all into their hands, and oftentimes give money for it aforehand, and make of it a *manipolium* (*sic*)? Who gaineth thereby? King Philip's subjects. And who is damaged thereby? All nations: because spices being in few mens' hands, they sell it as they themselves will, to the most of their own private profit, and to the hurt of all other.

Art. 8

Now, for the Spanish trade and the merchants of Spain, because they be King Philip's subjects, there is little to be said. But yet, I will somewhat declare how the Spaniards decay. The merchants of Antwerp be of such great wealth, that they be able to sell their commodities that make for Spain and the Indies to the Spaniards, at such high and dear prices, for long days of payment, that when his days of payment be come, and

[5] Cloths of medium weight and size, as defined by stat. 5 and 6 Ed. VI, c. 6.

the Spaniard lacketh the return out of the Indies and Spain, to keep his credit then he runneth upon interest or the exchange till return come; and by that time his gains is eaten out, and oftentimes a great part of his principal. Thus the Antwerpians shear the Spaniards yearly by selling them their worst commodities aforesaid. And their best commodities they themselves send into Spain; and do occupy more into Spain than all the Spaniards do. Thus all the gains and profit comes to Antwerp, and remaineth in the Netherlands.

Art. 9

For the trade of the merchants of France: there hath been war so commonly betwixt the House of Burgundy and them, that by means therof there hath been great colouring[6] of goods used betwixt the one nation and the other. And so commonly and cunningly it hath been wrought between them, that the Antwerpians and other merchants of the Netherlands be now so privy and skilful in all the French tricks and trades as the French merchants themselves; and by that means, in time of peace they damage the Frenchmen much, by reason [that] they know their whole secrets and trade, wherby they serve Germany and Spain, the Netherlands, Portugal, Eastland and other places, of wares as the Frenchmen were wont to sell there themselves. The gains wherof the French loseth both to the decay of the merchants and also of the navy. Which gain the Netherlands getteth to the wealth and strength of their prince and country, and specially to the increase of their navy; which is so marvellously increased within this thirty or forty years that King Philip is the strongest prince in Europe by sea, except the Queen of England.

Art. 10

Now let us go to England, and see what the Netherlands hath done there. Truly, within this twenty-six or thirty years they have eaten out of London, being the head and principal city of that kingdom, the merchants of Italy, Germany and Spain, France and of Eastland, of every which nation there was in

[6] Smuggling, by a feigned ownership.

London divers famous and notable rich merchants and companies. And at this present few or none [are] left, except two Italians, one Spaniard and a few Easterlings. And of the Netherlanders at that time there were not above twelve or sixteen persons, and of those twelve or sixteen not passing four that were esteemed or taken as merchants, or did use any kind of merchandise. For all their merchandise that they brought into England was stone pots, brushes, poppets[7] for children, bristles for shoemakers and other such-like pedlars' ware and trifles; and sometime a little fish and three or four pieces of linen cloth. And now at this day, there are a hundred merchants of the Netherlands, wherof most or all be of Antwerp, that occupy England with all kinds of wares that the said merchants of strange nations were wont to bring; not only to the damage of the English merchants, but to the damage of all other merchants that were wont to occupy England. And truly, inasmuch as in them lieth, they seek only to destroy the English merchants and their trade, and have been many years about the same – which is now come to light and likely to make some great change, which were a happy thing to all merchants and nations saving to the Netherlanders themselves (if they would consider and weigh it well, how daily the Netherland merchants getteth their trade into their hands, to the enrichment of themselves, their prince and country, which is to the hurt, danger and disquietness of all other princes and states).

Art. 11

Now since I have talked so much in the trade of merchandise, I will declare how the said merchants of the Netherlands be entered into exchange[8] and delivering money by interest or, to term it plainly, by usury. Within this few years, there was no merchant of the Netherlands that knew how to deal or use the exchange. And now, they be at this present so perfect in the exchange, all the world through, that they deliver as much money for all parts as any other merchants do, both for Eng-

[7] Dolls.
[8] International currency exchange.

land, Spain and France, and also for all Italy through, and Germany and Eastland too, or any place else wheresoever that any exchange is used. And thus what trade is there of any nation or part of the world, wherinto they have not crept, and sought and gotten the knowledge of it, and trade and traffic thither, and almost eaten out all the merchants of the same?

Art. 12

What nation or merchants were wont to deliver money at interest, to serve princes and states in their wars or for other needful affairs? The German merchants were the principal, and some Italian merchants. And who delivereth most money now at interest? The merchants of Antwerp, and other merchants of the Netherlands. It is not much above thirty years past, that there were not above two or three merchants, at the most, of Antwerp that delivered money to interest; and they were not able to deliver £20,000, which is 80,000 thalers,[9] of their own proper goods. And now at this present, there are thirty or forty principal merchants able to deliver £300,000, which is 1,200,000 thalers, without any great hindrance or let unto their occupying. Besides these thirty or forty principal merchants, there are in Antwerp a great number of other mean merchants, and marvellous rich artificers, that be able to lend in manner as much more. All these be the natural merchants of Antwerp able to do, besides other merchants of the Base Country dwelling in Flanders, Brabant, Holland, Zealand, Artois and Hainault, that be able to lend £300,000 more. Here is about £900,000, which makes 3,600,000 dollars. All this money be the merchants, artificers and subjects of the Netherlands in time of need able to lend their prince, and not much hinder or hurt their occupying.

Art. 13

Now let us go to the 'common subsidy' or 'general gift', which is raised upon the lands and rents in the Netherlands, and not of mens' substance. This 'general gift' or 'subsidy' is named the Tenth or Twentieth Penny: wherin are com-

[9] See note, *supra*, 59.

prehended as well the rents of the houses within the towns or cities, as the lands and rents in the country. This gift or tax of the Tenth and Twentieth Penny amounteth to £350,000, which is 1,400,000 thalers; and this gift or tax of the said Tenth and Twentieth Penny, from the year of Our Lord 1544, the year wherin the last Emperor, Charles, and King Henry the Eighth of England agreed together to make war in France, which was the beginning of the great wars, which wars King Philip his son and Elizabeth now Queen of England ended about the year of Our Lord 1560, being sixteen year continued. Within these sixteen years' space, I say, the Tenth and Twentieth Penny was paid ten sundry times, which amounteth to the sum of £3,500,000, which maketh 14,000,000 thalers. And yet more than all this, within the said sixteen years all the Netherlands through, there was paid a Benevolence and Chimney Money; and this Benevolence was so much as every man would give the Emperor of his own free will towards the maintenance of his wars, which were marvellous sums. And so largely and bountifully his subjects dealt with him, that some one merchants gave him £1,000, which is 4,000 thalers. Now, this Chimney Money was, that for every chimney and place of any house through all his Netherlands where fire was made, or the place ordained to make fire in, the dweller paid 3*s.* 4*d.*, which is twenty Flemish stivers.[10] This Chimney Money, as I have heard said, came to £150,000; but I will but reckon £100,000, which £100,000 amounteth to 400,000 thalers. How saith your Graces, be not here incredible sums? And is it not an infinite treasure that this Base Country hath paid, and is able to pay and lend when the prince needeth? Are his golden Indies like unto these golden Netherlands, that within sixteen years have freely given their prince 14,000,000 and 400,000 thalers, which make £3,600,000 – besides all his tolls, excises, imposts and other duties?

Art. 14

Now, will you understand how his subjects have gotten all this treasure, whereby this prince and his country be so weal-

[10] Small silver coins.

thy? Let us, then, consider and see what merchandise there is in all Europe that is used to be sent abroad or transported from one region to another either by sea or land, whereof at one time or other, or at one place or other, at the first or last the prince, the merchant or the subject of the Netherlands hath not a gain and profit by it, one way or other: as the prince by his right and duties, the merchant by buying and selling, the artificer by his working, the shippers by transporting, the carrier or labouring man by his travail, and the husbandman by uttering his victual. Mark this well that I say: and the more you consider of it, the more you shall understand and find out how this great wealth cometh to enrich this prince and subjects.

And may not Emden, standing so commodiously as it doth, be made the like? Whereby such profit and riches may come to the imperial towns and subjects? Yes truly, in shorter time than the Netherlands have gotten their wealth. But now, to my purpose of the Netherlands. Oh you subjects of Antwerp and the Netherlands, what a milch cow be you to your prince! Truly, ye are the very tip and glory of all his wealth, power and state, as I will hereafter declare. And his golden Indies and Spain are not to be compared to you his Netherlands. Therefore, O ye princes and merchants of Germany and Eastland, behold, behold I say, and consider what a town you have of your own country, neighbour to both, named Emden standing in East Friesland, whose commodious river and haven, being the only quay and port of all Germany to the seas, is so good and fair that no river in Europe may be compared to it. So that you may of yourselves have any will unto it, you may, I say, reckon that [which] you have lost in strength and riches and dominion by sea and land, and bring the same wealth that Antwerp and the Netherlands do now enjoy to both the borders of Germany and Eastland, [ad]joining to East Friesland, to the great glory, honour and fame, and to the wealth and quietness also of the imperial state and subjects, and not live thus in bondage of a foreign prince as you do, as hereafter shall be declared.

Art. 15

Your Graces will say, that although strange merchants should depart from Antwerp, yet the commodities of the Netherlands be such, that of force they must go thither for them for that matter. I pray you, what commodities do the Netherlands so naturally and properly bring forth of themselves to make strange merchants so fain to come for them? But in short time I can tell you the way how the same commodities may be had and made in Emden as well or better, and as good cheaper or better, than they are to be had at Antwerp or in the Netherlands; and this shall be declared hereafter.

Art. 16

Your Graces will say, that out of King Philip's Indies there cometh such great plenty of gold and silver, that it sufficeth to buy up all the commodities that are either made or come into the Netherlands: and that the Indies have been the only furnishers of all, at least the most part of all, the gold in Europe: and [that] by the Indies King Philip and his Netherlands be made rich and not by the traffic and resort of strange merchants, as is alleged. I deny this point, and will prove that the Netherlands of King Philip be more profitable to him than his Indies (as is declared in the twelfth and thirteenth Article). And that by the Netherlands the trade of the Indies is maintained, and that all Christendom hath more damage than profit by the Indies, as for example thus: there cometh nothing from the Indies but a little gold and silver, and that is so dearly bought by [the] death and blood of so many Christian people that have been, and daily be, consumed in the getting thereof, some by the barbarous people, some with unwonted air, some by their meats and drinks being contrary to the Spanish diet and manner, some by very famine, some swallowed up and drowned in the seas by coming and going (as Spain can bear witness how many thousands daily do leave their bones there, to the great weakening of that country being a member of the Christian state): that in the reckoning how this gold is gotten, with trouble, I mean bloodshed, death and loss of Christian men to maintain and keep the state of those his Indies: what good nature is there, and pitiful Christian heart, that would not abhor to get gold in this sort? And God's law (we see) and Man's law both do forbid it. And now, to look upon the Netherlands, they get their gold quietly, without any such trouble or bloodshed; and maintain men, breed men and keep men. And by reason of the great traffic and resort of all nations thither, they bring into the Netherlands great quantity of gold ready coined, out of the Indies uncoined, as appeareth in the twelfth and thirteenth Article. So that his Netherlands be more profitable to him, as I said, than the Indies. And what do the Spaniards carry out of the Netherlands and Spain into the Indies, to that naked, idolatrous and idle people? Truly, so great abundance of all such necessary things, both of victuals and needful commodities, as the lack therof causeth a general dearth and scarceness of the same to be in divers places amongst many people and countries here in Christendom, and [is] well like to cause it more and more, so long as that trade is used. Aristotle and Theophrastus declare that the Africans and the people of Carthage had in times past found out that country, and trade thither for gold; but they show there withal, that by that trade they lost so many people that their state and country was much weakened by it. For they transported thither so much victuals and other commodities such as they could not spare, that soon there waxed a great scarceness and dearth of the same at home, even generally throughout their own commonwealth. But their princes and rulers, perceiving readily their lack, and wisely foreseeing what would soon follow if this trade into the Indies should be continued and maintained longer, for the speedy redress of the same they gave strait commandment and charge that there should no more ships go forth; nor people nor merchandise from thenceforth be sent thither any more. And for the bringing home again of their people that were then there, they sent empty ships and made general proclamations abroad throughout the Indies that all such as would return home should make themselves ready to take ships by a day, giving them understanding that after the return of those ships the Carthaginians would never traffic or send more ships again to that country. And thus was that trade utterly left off and never found nor used, until about the year of our Lord 1490 that noble prince Ferdinand, king of Spain, by his servant Christopher Columbus found it. And trust me in mine opinion, it were not amiss if that trade into the Indies were clean left off in these our days likewise, considering that the small deal of gold and silver that cometh from thence is in one prince's hand, and partly too the occasion of all the war and trouble that hath been in Christendom this forty or fifty years.

Art. 17

[W.G. *loq.*] Now, what will you say to the great number of woollen cloths that be made in the Netherlands, wherby so many thousands be set a-work? [Earl of East Friesland *loq.*] It is very true, there are many cloths made. [W.G. *loq.*] But from whence comes their wools? [Earl *loq.*] Out of England and Spain. But is not this Spanish wool then a natural commodity, by the reason that Spain and the Netherlands be under one prince? And can that Spanish wool be taken from them, that they shall not have it, neither to serve themselves nor to sell to their neighbours? [W.G. *loq.*] I confess, that Spanish wool cannot be taken from them, and that they make cloths therof at their pleasure. But, I pray you, what kind of cloth is it? Or how will it wear that they make of their Spanish wool alone, if English wool be not mingled with it? It is such cloth – and the experience of it is common – that he that proveth it once will not gladly buy of it again if he may get English cloth at a reasonable price. For Spanish wool endraped of itself maketh thick and greasy cloth, and being in a chest unworn, it either breedeth moths or consumeth of itself. And being daily worn, the staple or wool is so hard that it waxeth soon bare; and being bare, it will never abide the dressing again. Howbeit, if it be mingled with English wool, I must say it maketh indifferent good cloth to the wearing. So that I say, without English wool their cloth is little or nothing worth, without it be where none English cloth can be gotten.

Art. 18

[Earl *loq.*] Well, they make great abundance of tapestry, which serveth all Europe. [W.G. *loq.*] That is true; but from whence cometh all the stuff whereof their tapestry is made? [Earl *loq.*]

The wool cometh out of the land of Hesse in Germany, and out of England and Eastland; and the silk and gold out of Italy. [W.G. *loq.*] But you will ask me then, how shall I dye wools in colours at Emden or in these countries as good cheap as at Antwerp or in the Netherlands? I will tell you how: out of the land of Thuringia (which is not far from Emden), there cometh good woad. Besides, out of France it may be brought as good cheap to Emden by seas as to Antwerp. And madder is gotten in the East Country not far from Emden; and the country about Emden serveth well to breed madder. And alum cometh out of Italy, and may be brought as good cheap to Emden as to Antwerp. Copperas cometh out of Germany, and may be had much better cheap to Emden than to Antwerp. So that your Graces may see that both this stuff, and all other things that belongeth to tapestry-making (saving only the workmen) may be brought as good cheap to Emden as to Antwerp. And for the bringing of workmen to Emden, I shall hereafter show my advice.[11]

Art. 19

What say you to the making of says, worsteds, Bruges satins, mockadoes, and a great number of such kind of merchandise? I ask your Graces again, from where cometh this stuff but out of Germany, England, Eastland and Italy? From whence, they may be brought to Emden with all other things for making of the same, as I have declared for making of tapestry in this other Article, as good cheap as to Antwerp.

Art. 20

Your Graces will say, peradventure if they make many things of copper, copper wire, latten, brass, tin, iron and iron wire, and all such other hardware? I answer your Graces as afore, that all this stuff cometh out of Germany, Eastland and England, from whence it may be brought as good cheap to Emden as it may be to Antwerp; and wrought by the imperial subjects themselves to their own great profits, as well as it is at this day by the subjects of the Netherlands.

[11] *Infra*, arts. 55–9.

Art. 21

Your Graces will say, they make great store of linen cloth. It is very true. But a great part of their flax cometh out of Eastland. And yet in Westphalia, in the *stift* of Utrecht, Münster and Osnabrück, East Friesland, West Friesland and Groningerland, there is good store of good linen cloth made; and much more would be, able enough to serve as many as the Netherlands do now, if the marts were kept at Emden, to the great relief of many poor people that – I know – would gladly travail and make cloth, if they knew how to have utterance thereof so near unto them.

Art. 22

Your Graces will say, they get great store and quantity of madder. I grant it is true, that [it] is the best and only commodity that their country naturally bringeth out. And yet, it is of no necessity, by reason that madder is gotten in Germany and Eastland (as appeareth in the eighteenth article). Besides this, there are divers countries, as Groningerland, East and West Friesland, Gelderland and some parts of Westphalia and the *stift* of Münster, that have the like earth; and the ground serveth as well for madder as the country of Flanders, Brabant, Zealand and Holland. Howbeit by reason they lie so near to Antwerp, being the mart town, the makers of madder may deliver it better cheap there than those countries aforesaid can do that be far off, by reason that madder is heavy and troublous and chargeable to carry. But if the mart were kept at Emden, the said countries [ad]joining to it would breed, make, and in short time deliver plenty of good madder better cheap than the Netherlands are able to do. So that madder (you see) is no necessity, because it may and will be had and bred in other countries, to serve the same use that it is put to in the Netherlands.

Art. 23

Your Graces will say, they gather great quantity of butter and cheese in Holland. It is true, they do so. But all that which is gotten there, more than that which serveth that country of Holland, sufficeth not to help their neighbours and friends, as

Brabant, Artois, Hainault and Spain; for they have great quantity brought them out of East Friesland, West Friesland and Groningerland. And to come to talk of victuals, if East Friesland and West Friesland and Groningerland were not, how should they do for beef or oxen? Or for bacon, if Westphalia and Eastphalia were not? For they have not flesh half enough to serve themselves.

Art. 24

Thus your Graces may plainly see by these proofs, that the Netherlands of themselves do naturally bring forth neither victual to serve them, nor yet commodities of their own to gain and get this great wealth and riches they have. It is the resort of strange merchants, and the getting of other mens' trades into their hands, and the working of foreign commodities that come out of other countries (as you have heard) that makes their wealth so great. They get by all nations; but none can get or take any trade or commodity from them. For to say truth, they have nothing that is naturally and properly their own. But they set all their people a-work with the merchandise that cometh out of foreign countries unwrought, and so make divers kinds of small things; and specially of those commodities that come out of England, Germany and Eastland, wherewith their poor people in very deed be well set a-work, and many of them wax to be very rich. And as I have heard, there is not so few as 100,000 persons set a-work and fed in the Netherlands by the only working of foreign commodities. For the wool, cloth, lead and tin and other commodities that come out of England setteth a-work and maintaineth 50,000 persons, as hereafter shall be declared. What great help and benefit might this be to the imperial state and subjects to bring this occupying into the towns of Germany and Eastland!

Art. 25

But to my purpose again. If all strange merchants should leave the Netherlands, what merchandise is it, or other commodities, that may be said to be naturally and properly their own, that can induce men and draw men to come back again?

Or what is it wherewith they can set their people a-work within their own country, saving with Spanish wools? Whereof I have declared already the discommodity and inconvenience in the wearing, so that by this, thus much I prove: that forasmuch as almost all those things wherupon their Netherlanders do work do all naturally grow in England, Germany and Eastland, and in time may be as well made in Emden and in other towns thereabout as at this time they be in the Netherlands; that [activity] once removed and taken, all the strange merchants from them with their commodities [gone], they shall have nothing of their own to set their poor people a-work. And then, what will they be? Trust me, such as of nature they are, very naked: I mean, barren and poor. And thus their great wealth is grown, you see, plain by the resort and traffic of strange merchants, and by the working of those commodities that come from other nations, and of nothing they have of themselves or of their own.

Art. 26

Your Graces will perchance ask me, is any so meet a place within the Empire, standing so commodiously and so indifferently to work and make all these things in, and for all merchants to travail and resort to by sea and land as Antwerp, although these commodities before remembered be neither naturally nor properly bred within the Netherlands? This matter is soon answered. That is: your city of Emden in East Friesland, an imperial city that stands more commodiously than Antwerp doth to the seas, having the best and fairest river in Christendom for all merchants to pass and re-pass with their ships and goods. And having a good wind, it is not above twenty-four hours' sailing further from England, France or any other country or region westward than Antwerp is; and the river of Ems and that coast is much better to fall with than the coast of Flanders, Zealand, or the river of Antwerp. And besides this passage by water, there may be as good cheap and as commodious passage by land, both to and from Germany, Eastland and Italy to Emden as there is to Antwerp, which the English merchants have proved this summer true. So that you see that in short time Emden may be made as good a merchants' town as Antwerp is now, whereby all the imperial towns [ad]joining unto the same may be replenished and set a-work, with all kinds of cunning artificers and knowledge, if they please to lend their helps unto it.

Art. 27

Thus your Graces may see plain, how rich they be made by their traffic, and after what sort their riches are grown, and how soon the same wealth may be taken away if you and other imperial princes will vouchsafe to cherish the merchants, and specially the English merchants and their commodities that come unto you. But besides this infinite wealth that resteth now among King Philip's merchants and subjects of the Netherlands, I purpose to declare what great wealth and treasure even of the subjects of other princes and nations he hath by very policy in manner as much at his command, as that, that belongeth properly to his own subjects. And with that, I will show you how dangerous and hurtful this wealth and treasure of his is to all the state of Europe, being in his hands as it is. And then, I will declare mine opinion withal for the taking away of this traffic, which shall not only impoverish them sore by placing the same in Emden, being an imperial city; but also readily redress these dangers and cause great quietness, profit and assurance to ensue to all the state of Christendom, and specially to the whole Empire and princes of the same.

Art. 28

Besides this wonderful wealth that the subjects of King Philip have gotten by strange merchants and nations remaining in the Netherlands at King Philip's commandment, he hath also the most part of the treasure of the richest merchants in Germany, Eastland, Italy and Spain, and the substance of many merchants of England in like manner, by their dwelling in Antwerp and other places of his Netherlands with their goods and the goods of divers other (being in their hands by commission), as much at his command in a manner as the goods of his own natural subjects. For the Spaniards be his own natural subjects. The Italians, as they of Naples, Milan and other parts of Lombardy and Savoy, they be all his subjects. And the rest of the Italian merchants, except the Venetians, by reason of the Pope's league with the House of Spain and Burgundy (of which league I will speak hereafter), be as it were his subjects. The merchants of Eastland and Germany be so planted in the Netherlands, some by marriage, some by buying of lands and houses (as hereafter I shall tell you), that they be affected as much to that country as to their own, by reason that the most part of them have wives, children, houses and lands, in a manner all their substance, there.

Are not the Fuggers (being German born, and the richest merchants in Europe or, as I think, in the world) with the most part of their substance by policy planted in King Philip's countries? And hath he not caused them for such debts as he and his father the Emperor Charles owed unto them, to take lands in Spain? By the means wherof he hath gotten at his command not only the treasure of the Fuggers, but also all the rest that these our German merchants have in Germany, so that they dare not once displease him or deny him anything soever that he requireth? Mark what help it is that Germany, their own natural country, were like to have of them if need were: no help by them, but hurt by them. Is not the company of Welsers, the company of Pimels, Conrad Rehlinger, David Langenmantel and his company, Hans Oertel and his company, Jeronymus Oyer (*sic*) and his company, Othmar Ridler, George Spavenberger (*sic*) and his company, Martin Schönecker and his company, the heirs of Lazerus Tucher, Lazerus Rantzau, the company of Schorers, Andreas Imhof, Christopher Ingold, with divers other which I do not reckon, planted in Antwerp? The most part of these have married Netherlands women and have children, houses and lands, and are become subjects, as it appeareth.

For they did obey King Philip's proclamations and commandments. And either for the love they bare to Antwerp and that country, or else for the fear they were in at that time, being in King Philip's danger, they would not, or durst not, come to the town of Emden to buy the English commodities as they were wont to buy [them] at Antwerp; nor yet, send to Emden such German commodities as English merchants were wont to buy of them at Antwerp. But rather, unnaturally not willing to help or further their country, some of them sent their merchandise to Antwerp and from thence into France, to their unreasonable charges; and from thence into England, where they were not so well sold, reckoning the great charges they were at in sending to and fro, as they might have been at Emden: doing by this as much as was in their power to overthrow the begun trade at Emden. So that now, if it would please your Graces to look well into these things, ye should easily see that if war should break out betwixt the Empire and the House of Burgundy or Spain (as God defend), that all these, being German merchants, with their own proper goods, which is worth £800,000 or £1,000,000, besides their persons, and other goods of German merchants being in their hands also, would be good prize to King Philip; and with these goods, you see, he might easily long maintain his wars against you.

But these goods and the merchants, if the marts were kept at Emden or at some other imperial city, would be out of such dangers and always ready within the Empire to the defence of the imperial state against all enemies. But these Burgundians do by little and little so *politiquely* (*sic*) pluck such feathers, not only from the noble eagle as well by countries as towns and subjects (as that, unless it be looked unto in time, when she thinketh to fly, she shall be in danger to fall), but also from other princes and states besides, not only part of their countries and towns but also their most wealthy and richest merchants and subjects, that by the means of this traffic they have always so much foreign substance in their own hands that it maketh them still, as in times past it hath done, more insolent and bold to proffer wrongs and injuries to other princes and countries, their neighbours and friends, by the reason they have their subjects and goods in their hands.

And thus, all the merchants of most countries in Europe except England and France do inhabit and dwell, and have most part of their substance that is in Europe, in King Philip's countries, and be as his subjects. And yet, the English merchants be not wholly departed from Antwerp. But indeed, such order is taken in England of late, that they must depart by a day, or else become Burgundish and then lose all their privileges and freedoms and never after be taken again as Englishmen. Thus your Graces may see, where merchants be there is always plenty of money. And all the best and richest merchants in Europe be in King Philip's Netherlands at his command. Then is most of the treasure in Europe at his command, you may see. And thus is he made the richest prince in Europe with the subjects and goods of other princes and nations: which is a dangerous matter and a lamentable case, that he may at all times when it pleaseth him stay money from what prince he will, or let the money to what prince he list. And yet, by right most part thereof belongeth neither to him nor to his subjects; and money makes him so rich and strong that unless it be shortly foresworn it will be too late to redress it, as hereafter it shall be declared.

Art. 29

Now may your Graces and other imperial princes see, where and in whose hands and by what policy the greatest part of the treasure in Europe remaineth. Then let us consider how this treasure hath been used in times past, and how it is used now at this present, and how it may be used in time to come. And likewise let us consider how this great and mighty prince King Philip is settled, having this great treasure at his commandment; and what great countries, towns and cities his father the Emperor Charles hath gotten with the treasure of his Netherlands and left to his son King Philip, who to this day keepeth them still. Whereof part be imperial and of late time be almost degenerate and become naturally Burgundish. Wherein is much to be noted and considered what may follow, whereof I will be so bold [as] to declare mine opinion.

Art. 30

With this great treasure, did not the Emperor Charles get from the French King the kingdom of Naples, the dukedom of Milan and all other his dominions in Italy – Lombardy, Piedmont and Savoy? With this treasure, did he not take the Pope prisoner and sacked the see of Rome? With this treasure, did he not take the French King prisoner and maintain all the wars with France since the year of our Lord 1540 to the year of our

Lord 1560, as is declared in the twelfth and thirteenth article of this book? With this treasure, hath he not maintained many cities in Italy as well against the Pope as against the French King, as Parma, Florence and such other? With this treasure, did he not overthrow the Duke of Cleves and take Gelderland, Groningerland and other dominions from him? Which ought to be a good warning to you all, as it shall be most plainly and truly declared hereafter. With this treasure, did he not get into his hands the earldom of Lingen in Westphalia? With this treasure, did he not cause the Earl of Esens, your subject, to rebel against your Graces' father and against you, the cause you know best? And what work this treasure made amongst the princes and towns in Germany when the Duke of Saxony [and] the Landgrave of Hesse were taken, Sleidan our own countryman by his *Chronicle* declareth at large.

And did not this treasure, named the Burgundish ass, walk and run in all places, to make both war and peace at pleasure? And took he nothing from the Empire then? Yes, truly, too much, as you shall hear. When the Emperor Charles was first made Emperor, what were the towns and countries in the Netherlands that justly or properly came to him by birth or inheritance? There was Brabant, Flanders, Holland, Zealand, Artois and Hainault. And yet, there is a great question concerning Holland, how the Emperor Charles and his progenitors came by it, and what homage or duty they ought to do for the same; because thereby the House of Burgundy hath the mouth of the river of Rhine at his commandment, which is to the great loss, damage and danger of Germany, as hereafter shall be declared. Here be all the countries that belong there to the House of Burgundy when the Emperor Charles was made Emperor. But how much hath been added to the Netherlands since by him, contrary to his oath made? These are these towns and countries, as it appeareth in the Sleidan's *Chronicle*, viz: Luxemburg, Limburg, Gelderland, the earldom of Zutphen, the city and the *stift* of Utrecht, with all the lands over the Yssel, West Friesland, the city of Groningen and Groningerland; and as before it is said, he hath by policy gotten into his hands the earldom of Lingen standing in Westphalia, and by the like policy, with money he is become the defender of the earldom of Esens, which is parcel of your Graces' country of East Friesland. All these countries and towns, with the treasure of the Netherlands hath he taken from the Empire.

Art. 31

Your Graces will say, that all these be imperial countries; that always and at all times they have been and yet be under the government and commandment of the whole empire. It is true they were so, about thirty years past. But, since that time, the Emperor Charles with his great riches and treasure of the Netherlands hath joined them to the House of Burgundy; whereof some he took by force, some by policy, and some others he got by fair speech under colour and name of being their defender, promising them they should hold all their customs, liberties and freedoms. But having so gotten them once into his hands, he hath in this time made them now, contrary to his other promise, as natural subjects unto him as any his Netherlands be, as well by paying all duties unto him, as obeying all the Burgundish proclamations and commandments. Thus by little and little, the Burgundish bind fast and make sure all things that come into their hands. And have they not long practised to make a fort or castle in the town of Groningen? Which if they could once obtain, were not that town and country in the like case that the city and *stift* of Utrecht is in? For if they could once get a fort or castle built in the city of Groningen, then were it time for East Friesland and the river of Ems to take heed: which is the only port to the sea of all the Empire. And also you earls of Emden, and the ancient and noble earls of Oldenburg and the duke of Lüneburg and other princes their neighbours, and also you bishops of Münster and Osnabrück in like manner have cause to take heed for the *stift* of Münster and Westphalia; for then shall the river of Ems, the only part of the Empire, be taken from you, and your countries be in great danger. For King Philip is already entered as aforesaid into Westphalia by the earldom of Lingen, and into East Friesland as a defender of the earldom of Esens.

A wolf will be as profitable a shepherd to sheep as the duke of Burgundy a profitable defender to any towns and countries belonging to the Empire. Therefore I say to your Graces, take heed, you princes of East Friesland and other imperial princes, for King Philip hath as much treasure or more than his father the Emperor Charles had, and hath long gone about and sought means to get the river of Ems and East Friesland into his hands, to bring to pass that thing his father the Emperor Charles long desired. As read the eighteenth book of Sleidan's *Chronicle* and there your Graces shall see by the Emperor's own confession to the French King's ambassador how continually, [for] twenty years long, he sought the way and means how he might conquer Germany and join it to his House of Burgundy – which can never be, so long as the river of Ems and East Friesland be imperial.

But if he should once get into his hands this country and river, what could Germany have from the seas to relieve their country withal? Or what foreign prince, being friend to Germany, could come by seas to aid or help them, if they had need? What new tolls, excises and other imposts might the Burgundish Prince (if he would) [have] of all things that come by seas into Germany, if East Friesland and that noble river Ems, the only jewel to the Empire, were under the House of Burgundy? Which way could you imperial princes have any things from the seas, either by the river of the Rhine or the river of Ems, which of right be both your own, but you must have it by the licence of the House of Burgundy? Wherefore I say unto your Graces, mark what danger you be wrapped in, [you] that had two notable and famous rivers to the seas named the river of the Rhine and the river of the Ems, whereby the Empire and the subjects might have had ever free passage and course to and from the seas at all times at pleasure, into or out of any place of the world that is travelled by ship. The one of these two rivers named the Rhine is gone from you, by reason [that] it runneth into the seas through Holland – being King Philip's country, who may stop it at his pleasure from you, as he did this year of our Lord 1564, that no goods might go to or from Emden into Germany. The other is the noble river of Ems which is yet imperial, but in danger to be Burgundish unless you look well to the city of Groningen and Groningerland, in which city and country (as I have declared) consisteth only the imperial liberty to and from the seas.

Wherfore it had need to be well looked to, for if King Philip build a fort in that town, as he and the Burgundish of long time have most earnestly sought and do yet still seek, King Philip will then by little and little build upon the river of Ems such forts and castles that no ship shall be able to come to Emden. And then hath the Empire wholly lost all the free passage to and from the seas and so shall be shut up in a corner, that no traffic can neither come nor go to or from them, to their great danger and hindrance. And this river being once in the Burgundish hands and government, it cometh not lightly out again. Then is the imperial state and the princes thereof compassed round about by the House of Burgundy both by sea and land, [so] that no foreign help can come to them by sea. They have compassed you from all your ancient friends and neighbours of England, France, Scotland and Eastland. And by land, they have compassed you with the House of Burgundy of one part and the dukedom of Milan, the kingdom of Naples, the Pope and Italy of another part. And then his cousin-german and brother-in-law Maximilian the King of the Romans and likely to be emperor, and yet heir apparent to King Philip (if that sick child the Prince of Spain should die): this Maximilian, I say, with his kingdoms of Hungary and Bohemia and with his dukedom of Austria, doth compass you again with another part. Besides this, there is yet standing neuter, and very doubtful if any need were, the *stift* of Utrecht, Limburg, Luxemburg and other towns and countries before written that were once imperial. And whether they now be Burgundish or imperial hereafter, of that I will declare more. Therefore, consider these things well: in what danger the imperial state is and likely to come to, by suffering the House of Burgundy by little and little thus to creep into the Empire.

Art. 32

Your Graces will say that although East Friesland and the river of Ems were Burgundish, yet the imperial state and subjects might be relieved and have passage both to and from the seas by the rivers named the Weser and the Elbe, running by Bremen and Hamburg into the seas. No, truly, they cannot. For if Ems and East Friesland were Burgundish, Bremen,

Hamburg, Oldenburg, Lüneburg and the rest of these small earldoms, with Westphalia, the *stift* of Münster and Osnabrück would follow. For King Philip might not only famish part or most of them by hunger, in keeping corn, saltfish, butter, cheese and other victuals from them; but he might also make that your imperial princes and subjects should not be able to send out of their country wine or other commodities to foreign places, that of force must pass by water. For King Philip hath by policy gotten the earldom of Lingen into his hands, which stands in Westphalia upon the river of Ems and keepeth presently a garrison of soldiers there, which divers times hath been complained of at imperial councils and meetings; but as yet, no redress. And (as I myself have heard his officers say) he meaneth to build a strong castle there. And what could Bremen or Hamburg do then against this mighty prince, when they were thus cut off from the Empire both by sea and by land, but be in quietness and glad to put their necks in the Burgundish yoke?

And therefore, take example betimes by the loss of Holland and the river of Rhine, that the like come not to the river of Ems in East Friesland; and let Groningen and Groningerland take heed by the example of the *stift* of Utrecht and those towns belonging to it, which before the Burgundish had aught to do with them were as free as any part of the Empire. For notwithstanding all the Burgundish fair promises, the said towns in the *stift* of Utrecht do pay excise for all things, and imposts with other new payments which they never paid nor knew in times past. And doubtless in short time they shall be further compelled as Holland is now; which ought to be free, and was free till now about the year of our Lord 1552, at which time they were first compelled to pay the Tenth and Twentieth Penny perforce, both against the law and also the promise and oath of the Emperor and King Philip his son. For neither oath made by the prince, nor old customs, or written privileges, would serve to keep their liberties and freedoms. But of force they are compelled to pay, as often as the Netherlands do, all manner of excises, imposts, loans and gifts, named the Tenth and Twentieth Penny. And so shall West Friesland and Groningerland and other countries be sure to do; and in time they shall be as the Hollanders be, natural Burgundish. For truly, I myself travelling [in] those countries late imperial about my affairs, in asking the people whose subjects they were and under whose government they lived, they said they were King Philip's subjects and under the House of Burgundy, and almost think [it a] scorn to be called German or imperial, and specially the youth.

Art. 33

Well, mark what will follow within this twenty or thirty years to come, when all these old folks shall be dead and gone that dwelt in these countries and were once good imperial subjects, and knew their liberties and freedoms before the House of Burgundy had any commandment or jurisdiction over them; and that none shall be living but those that shall be born since that time, and brought up from their childhood ever under the Burgundish laws, orders and obeisance. What will they be? Let your Graces think; when for no matters of law, wrongs or judgments, by your own consents they cannot nor may not appeal to the imperial Chamber (which naturally is and ought to be their place of judgment), but must go to Brussels and have all their judgment of the House of Burgundy. Which bondage and loss of liberty in giving over the imperial people from the judgment of their own natural prince, countrymen and laws, to be judged by a foreign prince and his laws and people, in mine opinion is not well but injurious many ways, and truly giveth them just cause to be natural Burgundish.

And likewise, if any discord or war should fall out betwixt the House of Burgundy and the Empire (seeing there be under the Burgundish obeisance laws and judgments) to become also natural friends and true subjects to the House of Burgundy, and natural enemies to the imperial state and subjects, because you have given them or, as I may term it, rather sold them to the Emperor Charles, and put them for a little money under the yoke of the House of Burgundy. Thus your old friends and good neighbours and natural subjects that were once the frontier of your country, and always in the teeth of the Burgundish, and ever a scourge, as it were, unto them whensoever there was any need, be now changed by your means and sufferance;

and of old friends and good neighbours are become new enemies now, and ill neighbours; and of natural subjects I may say natural enemies and strangers. And where they and other stranger towns together were sometime the strength and frontier of the Empire, and always in time of need a scourge to the Burgundish and in their teeth, now be they and their strong towns the frontier of the House of Burgundy, and in time of their need will be a scourge, and in the teeth of the imperial subjects.

Art. 34

Your Graces will say not so, for that all these towns and countries he holdeth but only by composition of the Empire and doth his homage for them at every emperor's coronation: and look what these towns and countries were wont to pay and answer the empire for all contributions and gifts to maintain war against the Turk and all other imperial enemies. King Philip answereth and payeth double as much for them to the emperor, you will infer therupon; so that, that there is rather a great profit grown to the Empire by this means. To answer this point, trust me if it shall please your Graces, to look well into it. And mark it well: you shall find a small profit in it, to sell as it were, and give over so many princely towns and countries, and valiant and worthy people (whereby the imperial state is so much weakened) for a little money. Your Graces may well consider that King Philip payeth not that overplus of money that he priseth of his own charges: but that he raiseth it again by new imposts and other new exactions that he layeth upon them, as it is said of Holland and Utrecht, and that he gathereth a marvellous sum more than he payeth. And trust well unto it, that in the end, when by continuance of time they be made his faithful subjects and that they have forgotten all the imperial liberties and their allegiance that of duty they owe unto the Empire, he will deny all promises made unto you and the Empire, either in contributions of money or for aid of men to withstand the Turk or otherwise defend the imperial causes. And with such money as he will be able to raise of those countries and towns, he will maintain his war against you when he seeth his time.

And thus as I have said (which is the most dangerous matter of all), by tract of time and very policy he maketh them his natural subjects, whereby in time to come this Burgundish prince shall be able to gather great armies of good soldiers together either to serve against the Empire or other his enemies wheresoever, where before these imperial countries and towns were joined to the House of Burgundy (although the said House of Burgundy had great plenty of riches and treasure by such means as I have declared) yet they had no men of war, for the people of the Netherlands be no good soldiers; for in their time of need the Burgundish prince by request had his soldiers out of Germany and such as the imperial princes would permit them to have out of the Empire. And now you have suffered the House of Burgundy to have your country from whence came your best soldiers. Well, if these countries be not returned by some order to the Empire again, mark what will follow. Your Graces will answer that although these countries be at King Philip's commandment, yet he hath sworn and doth promise not to do anything that may be hurtful to the imperial state and subjects. And you think withal, perchance for all this, that they will not obey him in any such thing neither, although he would command them, considering he doth hold them but conditionally. Then and please your Graces, what say you to this matter that I shall speak of, and tell me whether it be obedience in them or not, or hurtful or no to the imperial state and subjects, and how King Philip observeth the oath he hath taken and made to the Empire.

Art. 35

Now this last summer, in the year of our Lord 1564, the English merchants, upon a variance between King Philip and the Queen of England, would come no more to King Philip's Netherlands with their ships and their merchandise, but came to your Graces' town of Emden to keep their marts there, and to buy and sell as well with the imperial merchants and subjects as with any other merchants of other nations. This town of yours of Emden (being an old and an ancient member of the Empire) ought to be free for all nations being in good amity with you and paying your Graces their accustomed rights and duties, as well to come and to go as to buy and to sell, and bring in and carry away all kinds of merchandise without restraint. But did not King Philip as king and only ruler of the towns and countries aforesaid [not] only keep the merchants of stranger nations and countries not being his subjects from Emden, but also his straight and sharp proclamations and commandments to all the towns as well within his Netherlands and also the towns and countries aforesaid that he holdeth of the whole Empire, that upon a great pain they should not buy up any English commodities at Emden to bring into any of his countries, towns or dominions aforesaid (that is to be understood, neither into the Netherlands nor into the countries he holdeth of the Empire), and that neither any of the towns or countries aforesaid should so much as dare upon the like pain to carry any commodities made in their countries to Emden, nor yet sell them to Englishmen nor to merchants of Emden, being imperial subjects?

But went he not further? Would he so much as suffer strange merchants, not being his subjects, to carry to Emden such goods as they brought out of their own countries to Antwerp? Or else to buy goods in Antwerp to carry to Emden to sell to the imperial subjects, although the said goods were neither made nor did grow in his Netherlands, nor could not come to his Netherlands but through Germany or Eastland, and by the sufferance of the German and Easterly princes and towns? These princes, iwis,[12] if they would be so strait to King Philip as King Philip is to them, what goods could come into his Netherlands? But in the time of the most cruel wars that were between France and the House of Burgundy, might not the merchants of Germany, England, Eastland and Italy, being in Antwerp and having amity with the House of Burgundy, might not, I say, the said merchants buy in Antwerp and in the said Netherlands all kinds of merchandise and carry the same into their countries, and having it there, [be able] freely to sell it to all nations without exception that would buy the same, were they Frenchmen or other? Or when the war was between

[12] Indeed.

France and England, did not King Philip's subjects and merchants of the Netherlands being in England buy up English commodities and carried them over to Antwerp and other places in the Netherlands, being in amity then with England, and freely sell the same goods as well to Frenchmen as other merchants that would buy it? And though it should be war (which the Lord of his mercy defend) betwixt England and the House of Burgundy, should not the merchants of Germany, of France, of Italy and Eastland buy all kinds of goods in Antwerp and the Netherlands, being in amity with them, and carry the same goods into their own countries, and there freely sell the same to what nation or merchants that would buy it, were he English or other? How saith your Graces to this point? Is this obedience in them, or no? And how observeth King Philip his oath taken and made to the Empire? Is not this a hurtful thing to the imperial state and subjects, to let and hinder the traffic that should come unto the imperial towns? As though no countries, merchants or nations ought to trade in any place but in his country; and when and where and with whom it pleaseth him to maintain still all the whole trade of merchandise in his Netherlands alone. By his commandment upon penal laws to forbid and keep the imperial merchants and subjects from occupying, buying and selling within the Empire, as though he were an emperor, it is not only a mere wrong to the whole state of the Empire, and great loss and damage unto the people, who for lack of such commodities as Englishmen to bring and carry away to and from such places as they traffic unto, do live without work – poor artificers I mean, by whom towns be much maintained. But also in this point besides, King Philip touched near the type and honour of the Emperor and the whole Empire, taking upon him (being but the duke of Burgundy and in those matters a subject to the Emperor) to command, forbid and break the old and ancient freedoms and liberties which the whole Empire hath freely given and so long maintained and kept to all the subjects and friends of the same.

Art. 36

Well, doth your Graces now think that this is a matter to be suffered, that contrary to his oath made to the Emperor, King Philip should thus openly dishonour and wrong the imperial state? No, truly; but if this be quietly put up and suffered and no redress sought, you shall not only give him stomach and courage to attempt and command greater matters than these against you and your countries, towns and subjects, which perchance you little think of at this time. But you shall by this example besides embolden other princes, your neighbours, to attempt the like when time serveth them; as for example, France for Metz, which town when it was demanded of the French king that it might be set at liberty according as it ought, answer was made that when the House of Burgundy delivered such towns as they had taken from the Empire, he would deliver Metz. This sharp attempt would have a sharp repulse, lest a slow repulse bring sharper attempts and bolden him to take from you all that he can get into his hands, and to hold and keep nothing that he hath promised to you and to the Empire longer than he seeth his advantage, and make him by policy (under divers colours of friendship) to eat up still, as it were, the imperial countries, towns and peoples with their ancient freedoms, liberties and customs. Wherefore I, being as I am a natural, poor, freeborn and a true imperial subject to your Graces and East Friesland, and one that sorroweth for the state of Germany and the imperial princes and the commonwealth and liberties of the same, I do most humbly beseech your Graces and other imperial princes, that like as your most noble and famous ancestors and forefathers were natural lovers of their countries and careful for the commonwealth and prosperity of the people, that you will in like manner have a natural regard and care to keep Germany and the whole imperial state in his old ancient freedoms, liberties and customs, the which by their great power and wisdom your noble ancestors have always worthily maintained and kept under the government of German princes from the time of Charlemagne the great Emperor to these our days (which is 797 years ago or thereupon by the computation of Carion and other writers), and not only continued the state thereof in great wealth and honour, to the immortal fame of the German princes and people; but also left with you their successors and heirs, for the maintenance of the same, good rules and order made and ordained by Otto the Third of that name Emperor, who reigned about the year of our Lord 974, which by reputation of the said Carion is about 690 years past. This same Otto for his singular wisdom, valientness and virtue, was named the world's wonder. And these orders and rules of his, made for the quiet election, government, continuance and maintenance of this Empire, if you imperial princes will faithfully and justly observe and keep, and withal cherish your countries, towns and subjects, and defend and keep them in their right freedoms and liberties, and maintain the foresaid traffic of merchants, you shall be easily able to command all princes in Europe, and not be commanded of any of them as you be.

Art. 37

[Earl of East Friesland *loq.*] Truly, these be great matters which you have opened and showed unto me touching the imperial state and the house of Burgundy and the Netherlands of King Philip, that by nature are very barren and poor, and yet by policy made rich and plentiful. [W.G. *loq.*] By the means whereof, the princes and people of the same be grown to an incredible wealth and riches in short time, what by the resort of strange merchants with their goods and merchandise as it appeareth, and specially by the amity of the English princes, and resort of English merchants and the commodities of England, in such sort as the said subjects and princes of the Netherlands have not only gotten into their hands almost all the trades and wealth of all the merchants of Europe, but are also become so rich and mighty that they have gotten from the Empire and other princes by divers means and policies their countries, towns and governments, the which King Philip keeps and makes as it were his natural patrimony and subjects. So that he is at this time, I may say, both the mightiest prince in Europe in dominions by sea and land, and also the richest prince in treasure: as well of that, that properly belongeth to his own subjects, as of that, that is at his command of the treasure of other princes' subjects which he hath always, as it were, in his hands. And then, considering how he is settled round about the Empire by sea and by land with his dominions and friends, and how he hath all this treasure at his command, I cannot see how the imperial state and other princes are able to get their own again without it be by open war, which would not only cause great taxes of money to be levied, to the great grief and grudge both of the imperial and other princes' subjects to maintain the war, but it would also make many factions and set much discord and civil war amongst the German princes themselves and make a great dearth and scarceness of all things in all countries: besides the trouble, disquietness and bloodshed that would ensue in Christendom throughout, considering that Burgundy and all the Netherlands are King Philip['s], and a great part of the Empire by sea and land (as you have heard declared in the thirtieth article of this book) likewise is at his command. Also the dukedom of Milan and some other parts of Lombardy and Savoy by friendship is his, and the kingdom of Naples, Sicily, Majorca and Sardinia and other islands thereabout Italy be, and the kingdom of Spain and the New Indies also. And that Maximilian the king of the Romans, Bohemia and Hungary, and duke of Austria, and likely to be emperor is his cousin german, and by marriage his brother-in-law and in possibility to be heir to all King Philip's dominions (as is declared in the thirty-first chapter at large). Also the Pope [is] his assured friend, and divers other princes in Italy, as Florence, Ferrara, Mantua, Parma and other. [Earl of East Friesland *loq.*] Is not this then a mighty government? And were it not a shrewd matter to buckle with such a prince? [W.G. *loq.*] Yes, truly, and he is so much the more to be feared and doubted in that his strength is so great; and it stands your Graces upon, with the rest of the imperial princes and all other princes, with the more wisdom and greater care to foresee it in time. For all these dominions that you have heard rehearsed, except the kingdom of Spain and the Netherlands, his father the Emperor Charles hath gotten only with the riches of the Netherlands. As [you may] read in Sleidan's *Chronicle*, and your Graces shall see how all things have gone from time to time, and how the merchants of the Netherlands did always furnish the Emperor Charles his father with money to maintain his wars (as I have said in the twelfth and thirteenth article of this book). So that your Graces may see in what point the power and strength of the house of Burgundy standeth. But if you German princes would friendly and faithfully hold together in one, and but observe your laws as you should: how easy a matter were it for you to overthrow them clean! For all that they do is by money which they have gotten politically by strange merchants; and by the like policy it may be taken away from them again. For take away the intercourse of the strange merchants, and then their traffic is gone. And the wealth that his subjects have gotten will soon consume and decay, when they shall daily spend and get nothing. And their riches [being] spent, and subjects in the towns and the countries grown once more to be poor, all these dominions cannot be kept and holden together when the great wellspring of money is taken from them.

Art. 38

[Earl of East Friesland *loq.*] You have said well. But how will you bring this to pass without great expense, war, trouble and bloodshed? [W.G. *loq.*] In very truth, by policy to take this trade away from this mighty prince and to bring it into Germany, I must say, were the greatest service that any man hath done to the imperial state in many years. Yes, it is a thing that will easily be done, seeing that God of his goodness hath so happily sent you English merchants with their commodities to us. If the princes of Germany will agree together as I have said, and maintain the liberties of the imperial subjects, which shall neither cost them or their country either money or trouble, more than a few words and commandments. [Earl of East Friesland *loq.*] What words and commandments may these be? [W.G. *loq.*] That it would please the Emperor and the imperial princes by their proclamations and commandments to assure that all the imperial subjects, and other foreign nations and merchants being in amity with the Empire, may quietly and freely buy and sell, come and go into and out of your country of East Friesland and town of Emden with their goods and merchandise, paying the old and ancient customs, rights and duties without controlment and let of King Philip and the house of Burgundy, in such sort as they be against all reason, league or amity (as is declared in the thirty-fifth article). Likewise, if other imperial princes and subjects do raise no new tolls contrary to the old customs, as the bishops of Münster and Cologne did this summer, doing as much as in them lay to overthrow this [already] begun traffic, which men suppose was not done without the practice and procurement of the House of Burgundy, who are so afraid to lose their milch cow that they seek all the ways and means they can to let this traffic to Emden. These things being performed, I will by the English nation in short time pull all other nations away – if so the merchants of Germany will have any natural respect either to their country or to recover their trade that the Netherlands have gotten from them (as is declared in the fourth article), or have any respect to avoid the dangers declared [already] that they and their posterity may be in assurance with their goods and persons (as is declared in the eighteenth article), or else will come to Emden, where they shall buy English commodities better cheap of the English merchants than at Antwerp.

Art. 39

[Earl of East Friesland *loq.*] Well, herein will be a great piece of doubt, how to bring this matter to pass, considering how men be naturally inclined nowadays. [W.G. *loq.*] I pray, your doubt is that my doubt is whether the love to a man's natural country, to his friends, his commonwealth and posterity do take more place in the heart of man, or the desire of his private commodities and gains? What is the cause that your Graces doth put this doubt? because that you have heard declared in the twenty-eighth article how the Fuggers and many more of the best German merchants be so settled and placed in Antwerp and other places of King Philip's dominions and be in a manner subjects that it will be a hard matter to pull them away, and specially those that be married to the Netherlands women. I will readily answer this doubt this way: if the duty and the natural respect of the safeguard and wealth of their native country will not bring them from thence, then must the princes and rulers of the cities and towns whereof these private merchants be incorporate members have a respect unto their charge and government in the commonwealth, and order these private men [that] they must do as the Easterlings of the

Hanse Towns do, and as the merchants of England have done now of late, perceiving the dangers aforesaid. But what is that? They must, I say, forbid the German merchants to marry any strange women that are not born within the Empire; or at the least, if they will needs marry, cause and see that they dwell not and keep house with their wives in their country where they married them, nor keep any house in strange countries with their wife and family, but by factors. Thus they shall be sure to keep their rich subjects and treasure within Germany. [Earl of East Friesland *loq.*] Hath not the imperial state as much authority to make statutes and laws as England and Eastland for their commonwealth? [W.G. *loq.*] Yes, truly; and if the imperial state had done as the Easterlings did long ago and as Englishmen have done now of late, it had been happy for them and their country.

Art. 40

[Earl of East Friesland *loq.*] Well, methinks by your arguments and reasons, that bringing the English Nation and their commodities to Emden, if the imperial princes will defend the right customs and liberties of the empire, that many other nations would follow the Englishmen. [W.G. *loq.*] Truly, it hath been proved some times past by other places, and is as likely to do so now. [Earl *loq.*] I pray you, then, is the commodities of England of such value, profit and goodness that all nations desire it, or the English merchants do buy and carry so much foreign commodities into England, that for the sale thereof all strange merchants will come to them where they be? [W.G. *loq.*] Verily, your Graces hath justly read and declared the truth both of the profit that comes by the English commodities and the profit that cometh by English merchants in buying foreign commodities, which great and inestimable benefits and profits no nation knoweth but only King Philip and his subjects of the Netherlands. And that maketh them so loth to forgo them and to seek all the ways and means they can possibly to keep them from Emden, not forgetting the example of Bruges in Flanders, nor the nature of their barren country if merchants depart from it. For they know [that] if the English merchants keep their marts at Emden they lose their fairest flower of their garland and the very root of their wealth.

Art. 41

[Earl of East Friesland *loq.*] I pray you, what be the commodities that come out of England, and by what means be they so profitable? [W.G. *loq.*] I will show your Graces. There is every year shipped out of England by English merchants and other strangers merchants, a marvellous number of woollen cloths, of sundry names, sorts and makings as hereafter followeth. First, there is shipped 80,000 white cloths, besides coloured cloths of all sorts, as kerseys short and long, cottons, northern dozens, penistones and divers other kind of coarse cloths. Which 80,000 white cloths be worth one with another £600,000, and that is 2,400,000 thalers, all these cloths being white. To be dyed and dressed into colours of all sorts, the least cheap colour of any cloth costeth dyeing and dressing 20*s*., some cost 30*s*., some 40*s*., some £3, some £4, some £5, £6, £7, £8, £9, £10, and some more. So, reckoning the coarse cloths with the fine cloths together, at the least the dyeing and dressing costeth of every cloth 40*s*., which amounteth to £160,000 for workmanship only. Who getteth this money? Poor labouring men and artificers, as the dyer, the clothworker, the madder-seller, the alum and woad-seller, the copperas and gall-seller, and a great number more that I do not reckon; and after these 80,000 cloths be dyed and dressed, then the packer gaineth for his work, then the porter gaineth for carrying them two or three times, then the skinner gaineth for skins to pack with, the canvas-seller for canvas, the roper for ropes and thread, then the porter gaineth again after they be packed, then the weigh-master for weighing the packs, and then the carter that carryeth them into Germany to the marts of Frankfurt, Leipzig and Nuremberg and other places. So that there is spent by these petty charges on every cloth at the least 4*s*. 6*d*., which amounteth to £18,000, that is 72,000 thalers. All this is gained by artificers and labouring men, besides the merchants, who gain in every cloth 40*s*. before it come to wearing, which maketh £160,000, which is 640,000 thalers. So there is gained by these 80,000 white cloths, by the merchants, artificers and poor labouring men £338,000, which maketh 1,352,000 thalers.[13]

Art. 42

Now let us go to coloured cloths of all sorts (besides coarse and fine kerseys, long and short, northern dozens and colours, with all other kinds of coarse coloured cloths, which I reckon will be about 40,000 cloths coloured). And these be worth £8 a cloth one with another, which amounteth to £320,000 which is 1,280,000 thalers, the charges [for] dyeing, trimming and dressing these cloths [being] according to the nature and quality of the same. All which money [that] poor men get by labouring (besides the merchants) is at the least 13*s*. 4*d*. upon every cloth one with another; wherin I reckon the portage and carriage into Germany, Italy and other places, with the packing and such-like charges, cometh to £26,666 13*s*. 4*d*. which amounteth to 106,666 thalers, which maketh £26,666 13*s* 4*d*. (*sic*).

Sum[*ma*] *totalis* of the value of the woollen cloth that yearly cometh out of England, besides the charges of dyeing and dressing, [is] £920,000, as may appear, which make 3,680,000 thalers; of which cloths there is gained by the artificers and poor working men, and by the merchants that sell them, £444,666 which maketh 1,778,666 thalers. The merchants gain by the said cloths £240,000, which is 960,000 thalers.

Art. 43

Besides these woollen cloths, there cometh out of England lead, tin, saffron, beer, coney skins, leather, tallow, alabaster stone, corn, with divers other things, amounting to great sums of money. Whereby a great number of poor labouring men are set a-work and gain, besides the merchants, who get great and large sums of money thereby. Also of which charges and gains can be no just estimation nor computation made, so that I let it run into this reckoning for advantage. And also the money that shippers get by freight of their commodities aforesaid,

[13] See note, *supra*, 59.

which is a great matter if the particulars might be justly reckoned.

Art. 44

Now will I come to wools and fells that cometh out of England yearly into the Netherlands, which wools and fells be worth at least £100,000, which maketh 400,000 thalers. Which wools be endraped in the Netherlands, whereby are set a-work carders of wool, spinners, weavers, clothworkers, thickers of cloth, dyers and divers other that get money thereby sundry ways. Makers of parchment and glovers gain therby, of whose gains I am not able to make account but by this way: that I have heard English merchants of great experience say they make no cloth coloured in England, how coarse so ever the colours be, but the charges that goeth to the making of it, as spinning, weaving, dressing and dyeing with other charges before it be ready to be sold, costeth more than the wool costeth; and I dare say the Flemings and the Netherlanders can make no better cheap than the Englishmen do. So reckoning the wool to be worth £100,000, the artificers and poor labouring men get as much in making the cloth as is declared, [that is] £100,000 which maketh 400,000 thalers. What gaineth the merchants thereby then that sell these cloths, which may be by estimation about 34,000 cloths, so that reckoning every cloth but 20*s*. gained and it is £34,000. So here is gained by the poor labourers, artificers and merchants by wool that cometh out of England £134,000 which maketh 536,000 thalers. I will collect now and put together of what value both cloth and wool is that cometh out of England yearly to the Netherlands, and then how much more poor labouring people and artificers get by the sale thereof, whereby shall appear the profit that cometh by English merchants and by the commodities of England.

Art. 45

The value of woollen cloth and wool that yearly cometh out of England into the Netherlands, and how much the poor artificers, labourers and other poor people get by their labour and work, and how much the merchants gain by the same is as followeth:

The 80,000 white cloths be worth undyed and undressed	£600,000
The 40,000 coloured cloths, with kerseys and other coarse cloths	£320,000
The wool and fells unwrought be worth as is declared	£100,000
The whole sum of English cloth and wools yearly sent over amounteth to the sum of	£1,020,000
	which is 4,080,000 thalers

The poor artificers and labouring people gain by working these 80,000 white cloths	£160,000
The packers and carriers and such like gain by these 80,000 white cloths	£18,000
Gained by the 40,000 coloured cloths	£28,666
Gained by the working of wools and fells	£100,000
What artificers and labourers gain yearly by working English cloth and wools	£306,666
	which is 1,208,664 thalers

The merchants gain in the 80,000 white cloths, the sum	£160,000
The merchants gain by the 40,000 coloured cloths, the sum	£80,000
The merchants gain in the cloths made of the wools endraped in the Netherlands	£34,000
The gains which merchants gain yearly by the sale of English cloth is	£274,000
	which is 1,096,000 thalers

Here your Graces may see, the subjects of King Philip do gain yearly only by wool and woollen cloth that cometh out of England almost £600,000, which is 2,400,000 thalers, besides the gains they have by sundry other things that be of marvellous sums. How saith your Graces, is not here a profitable nation and commodity, wherby or by whom so much gain cometh yearly both to the poor people and merchants where the English merchants do traffic? Would not these gains both help the poor imperial people and enrich the merchants of Germany?

Art. 46

I will tell your Graces a matter that I do truly know. In the year of our Lord 1550, as appeareth in the 22nd book of Sleidan's *Commentaries*, [it is stated] that the Emperor Charles would have had the Spanish Inquisition in Antwerp and into the Netherlands. Wherabout was much ado, and neither the suit of the town of Antwerp nor of their friends could persuade the Emperor from it, till at the last they told him [that] if the Inquisition came into Antwerp and the Netherlands, the English merchants would depart out of the town and his countries. Upon which declaration, search was made what profit came by the English merchants. There was found by trial that within the town of Antwerp alone was 14,000 persons fed and maintained only by working of English commodities, besides the gains that merchants and shippers with other in the said town did get, which was the greatest part of their living, which were thought to be in number half as many more. And in all other places of his Netherlands, by endraping English wool into cloths, and by working other English commodities, there was 30,000 persons fed and maintained. This was the report given over to this mighty Emperor, wherby the town of Antwerp and the Netherlands were saved from the Inquisition. And as I have heard say often times both by English merchants and merchants of the Netherlands, that by the commodities that be brought out of England, and by commodities made in the Netherlands that merchants of England buy in the said Netherlands and carry into England, there is fed and maintained 60,000 souls, yea some have said many more. Now, as justly as I can, I have declared to your Graces the value and profit that cometh by commodities of England, and what profit the merchants, poor artificers and other subjects have thereby, besides four or five hundred merchants that have packhouses and chambers, wherby their rents be maintained, besides the great expenses the said merchants use otherwise.

Yet in all these other things passed, I have not said or reckoned anything what profit the prince hath by the toll, excises and other duties, wherof can no just estimation be made.

Art. 47

Now have I declared to your Graces what profits King Philip and his subjects of the Netherlands have by the English merchants and the commodities that come out of England, I will declare unto you what commodities the English merchants buy in Antwerp of all strange nations and of the Netherlands, and merchants of Antwerp, and carry the same commodities into England. And first I will begin with the High Dutch or German merchants. The English merchants buy of them Rhenish wine, fustians, cotton wool, copper, copper wire, iron, iron wire, copperas, latten, brass, kettles, steel, of all kinds of wares made in Nuremberg, harness of all sorts, guns, gunpowder, field pikes, running staves for horsemen. There is no kind of ware that Germany maketh or bringeth out but generally the English merchants buyeth as much or more of it as any other nation doth. All which things the German merchants may bring to Emden if they will, as good cheap as to Antwerp.

Art. 48

Of the Italians they buy all kinds of silks and specially of the finest and best velvets both wrought and unwrought, chamlets, fustians made in Italy, gloves, of all kinds of merchandise made in Italy. All which goods the Italians bring first from Italy to Cologne and so to Antwerp; and from Cologne to Emden it may be carried as good cheap as from Cologne to Antwerp.

Art. 49

Of the Easterlings the English merchants buy flax, wax, pitch, tar, wainscot, clapboard, deal board, oars for ships of all sorts, corn, furs, tallow, cables and cable yarn, masts for ships, soap ashes, hemp, estrich wool. There is no merchandise that cometh out of Eastland but serveth for England, and the English merchants buy it. And the Easterly merchants in coming to

Emden shall have most benefit thereby, for they shall not only save a great part of their adventure, travail, charges and loss of time that they be at in going to Antwerp, besides less adventure by seas; by reason [that] the coast of East Friesland and the river of Ems is much better to enter and fall with than the coast of Zealand, Holland, and the river of Antwerp.

Art. 50

With the Spanish and French merchants the English merchants hath not so much to do as with other nations, by reason that the English merchants occupy much into France and Spain, and so serve England from thence themselves.

Art. 51

But now let us go to Antwerp and the Netherlands and see what the English merchants buy of them: says, worsteds, mockadoes, linen cloth, fustians of Naples, striped canvas of all sorts, tapestry, Bruges satin, buckram, white thread, inkle, all kinds of laces made of thread or crewel, fustians made at Bruges, frisdaoes made of English wool, nails, all kind of iron work wrought, all kinds of things made of copper wire, latten, brass, iron wire, pins, knives, points, flax wrought, incredible sums of spicery that they buy of the contractors, hops I daresay 40,000 a year, all manner of pound work, named bands and laces for shirts, with other such things as English women use to wear upon their heads. If I would write all things that England spendeth and that the Netherlands make, I should make a book of that alone. But to make some kind of proof, [so that] your Graces shall perceive this infinite treasure that English merchants buy in Antwerp that England consumeth, you see in this book that I have made proof of the commodities that comes out of England to the Netherlands [which] is yearly worth £1,020,000 which is 4,080,000 thalers. And by proof made, the English merchants buy and bring out of the Netherlands into England of such merchandise as strange merchants bring thither, and such commodities as be made in the Netherlands, of a much greater value. And I have heard say, that all commodities that come out of other nations setteth not so many people a-work in the Netherlands as the commodities that cometh out of England doth; nor two nations that cometh into the Netherlands that buyeth and carryeth so much goods and commodities out of the Netherlands as the English merchant do. How thinketh your Graces now, what power, value and profit is the English merchants and the commodities of England, be they not worthy to be made (*sic*) cherished and desired, yea truly in my opinion more than any other?

Art. 52

[Earl of East Friesland *loq.*] And now you make me to remember one point or saying in your book, I think in the fourteenth article, which is: O Antwerp and the Netherlands, what a milch cow be you unto your Prince! [W.G. *loq.*] Methink it were truly spoken that the duke of Burgundy or King Philip should say: O my old faithful and profitable friends, you English merchants and the commodities of England, what a milch cow have you been always to my progenitors, and now to me and my subjects of the Netherlands. And truly no marvel although Bruges would give £100,000 to have the English merchants again, wherby they may get yearly almost £600,000. Neither is it [a] marvel though King Philip and his Netherlands be loth to depart from the English merchants, although for keeping them still in his country he should put himself in great danger as it is manifest he hath done already by his contempt[s] against the Empire, which, as you have said, are not to be suffered; although there came no commodity to the Empire by the withstanding of him, but only for our liberties' sake. But much more [it is] not to be suffered to bring this most profitable nation and their commodities to traffic with the imperial state and with the subjects.

Art. 53

[Earl of East Friesland *loq.*] But there is another thing that putteth me in some doubt: how Emden and the country therabout may be furnished of all kinds of artificers for making such number of necessary commodities as says, worsteds, Bruges satins, mockadoes, ironwork, and all manner of small things made of copper wire, iron wire, and such-like trifles as you have declared the English merchants buy in Antwerp, whereof many are more curious than necessary to serve the English merchants and other merchants that come to Emden. [W.G. *loq.*] Yes, these things by little and little in short time will be brought to pass, as I shall declare.

Art. 54

First, your Graces must consider the old proverb: Rome was not built in one day. Neither did the Netherlands get their great riches nor excellent knowledge in such arts as they now use. Therefore, seeing that within the imperial state Eastland doth not only and naturally breed and bring out the very substance of all commodities and artificial things that the artificers and subjects of the Netherlands do make, silk only excepted (which cometh out of Italy and may be had as good cheap to Emden as to Antwerp), but also [that] the imperial state, Eastland and England do naturally breed and bring out the most part or in manner all other compounds wherewith the said commodities be wrought and made in the Netherlands, and cannot be taken or kept from Emden [even] if the Burgundish would strive against this new traffic: thus having both substance wherof all these commodities be made and the things wherewith they must be made growing in the countries aforesaid, if your Graces and other imperial princes be willing, there may be set on work all the poor people in the towns [ad]joining near unto East Friesland, as Deventer, Kampen, Zwolle, Groningen, Osnabrück, Münster, Bremen, Lüneburg, Oldenburg and such other imperial towns, [which] may be replenished with all kind of cunning knowledge and artificers, as the towns in the Netherlands be; besides, all the countries therabout as husbandmen, by breeding all kinds of poultry, muttons, beefs and other victuals, shall have great gains. Rents both in town and country shall increase, and the husbandman of all things make money and wax rich; whereof always by one way or other the prince without his charges hath the most profit in all these things. [Earl of East Friesland *loq.*] You have satisfied me concerning the substance of all things thereof and wherewith the artificers do labour in the Netherlands, and that they may be brought to Emden as good cheap or better than to Antwerp. But I doubt me how the men may be gotten into those towns that should make these things. [W.G. *loq.*] Yes, they may be gotten four sundry ways.

Art. 55

First, your Graces must consider the artificer [who] liveth by his handy occupation; and if he make work that serveth only for England and cannot sell it, he cannot live. Neither can he live unless he may make work and sell it. Then if the English merchants who was (*sic*) wont to buy it be gone, it serveth for no man else. And when those artificers see their merchants gone from them into a new place or town where he may have the same commodities to work of as good cheap as at Antwerp to serve their merchants, they will for gain sake follow.

Art. 56

Secondly, your Graces knoweth all King Philip's countries through, his subjects use the Popish religion, in which his countries there is a great number of good Christian and religious people, that fear God, favour the Gospel and live thereafter, not without great fear and dangers daily both to lose their goods and lives. Which people be most cunning and expert in all those acts and occupations aforesaid, and to have liberty openly and freely to use their conscience, and so to instruct and bring up their children and family in the fear of God and the true knowledge of his word and commandments; and to be out of fear and danger both of losing their lives and goods; for religion['s] sake would be glad to come to East Friesland and other places therabout and set up all these arts aforesaid, wherby the subjects of that country and towns might learn the same. And no doubt but if the imperial princes had either by proclamations or otherwise seemed to have withstood this commandment of King Philip, whereby people that were and are willing to go from the Netherlands might have had hope of defence of this traffic, there would many artificers have been in the country and other imperial towns before this day.

Art. 57

Thirdly, they shall be able to keep their houses and families better cheap than in the Netherlands, by reason of the unmerciful excises and imposts, and great house-rents; and all other things appertaining to housekeeping is much better cheap in East Friesland than in the Netherlands.

Art. 58

Fourthly, they shall be free from the unreasonable taxes and payments, as the Tenth and Twentieth Penny, with such contributions as they were wont to pay there in the Netherlands when the prince commandeth, as appeareth in the twelfth and thirteenth article of this book.

Art. 59

And the better to bring these things to pass and good effect, your Graces and other princes into whose towns and countries these artificers shall come, considering the profit and benefit that shall ensue to your subjects and posterity and to the subjects of the Empire, [are advised] to grant unto the most needful and best occupations, as divers briars otherwise called Clothworkers, and such other, at their beginning some fordel[14] [of] freedom, liberty or help for certain years, to encourage them: as Nuremberg did for setting up of sundry arts in their towns, and [the] city of Ulm for making of fustians lent both great sums of money and gave other benefits to the beginners, considering the beginning of all new things at the first is harder and dangerous. Thus as I have said, the artificer knowing how to utter his ware, to have liberty of conscience for religion, and to keep his house, and live better cheap than he did, and to be free from great taxes and payments, and to have some help (as is said) at his first entrance: no doubt but in short time you shall bring most part of [the] artificers out of the Netherlands to your countries and towns to replenish them (as aforesaid) with all skilful concessions and necessary arts, to the great increase of your profit and maintenance of your country and towns both in rents, excises, imposts, tolls

[14] Parcel.

and other duties to the prince and subjects: and in time grow to that state and wealth that the Netherlands be. Wherby you shall weaken and pull down your strong and mighty neighbour both in treasure and subjects; which treasure and subjects when he shall lack, he will be as quiet and easy to deal with as other princes his neighbours, and as the princes of the House of Burgundy were three score and ten years past.

Art. 60

All these things must be done, as I have said, by cherishing and maintaining the English merchants, whose profitable commodities and traffic in buying and selling is largely declared unto you. Then, seeing that by God's ordinance they be come to your country being imperial, where not only they but divers merchants of other nations, which I know were minded to have come to Emden, thought no such sharp and strait commandment of the House of Burgundy should have taken place or been suffered to restrain or keep merchants from them, which caused them that they durst not come, but rather that the princes of Germany would as much have studied to keep and further them and all other merchants. And this traffic, considering the profit and assurance with the quietness that may come to the imperial state thereby, as King Philip studieth with the help of all his friends and daily seeks by divers ways and policies both to stay the English merchants and all other merchants of strange nations, which once were willing to come, from entering into traffic with the imperial subjects within the imperial state. Which proclamation and commandment of King Philip, if the imperial princes would withstand and maintain this traffic, do not doubt but, as I have said, without bloodshed or disquieting Christendom, even at this first beginning you shall pull away a great part both of strange merchants and traffic from King Philip's Netherlands, and in short time get the whole, and make your imperial country a pack-house for all merchants in Europe, as Antwerp and the Netherlands now be. Whereby your own subjects and merchants shall not only recover the trades that the merchants of the Netherlands have gotten from them, but also may traffic in their fathers' land, and their goods and persons be an assurance and at the imperial commandment in time of need, and in like manner all the goods and merchants of all other nations: whereby the whole Empire shall have a great profit, honour, wealth and strength, and command and not be commanded, and set great quietness amongst all Christian princes, and have the like advantage of all nations as King Philip and his subjects have now, as appeareth in the eighteenth article of this book.

Art. 61

Thus having within the Empire all the treasure in Europe, as Emperor Charles and King Philip of long time have had in their Netherlands wherewith, as I have declared, they have been troublers of all princes and states in Christendom: even so, you imperial princes having the same treasure in Germany shall be able to withstand the great and mighty tyrant the Turk, the most dangerous enemy to all Christendom, or any other imperial enemy. And also to correct and overthrow the evil life of that seditious and troublous tyrant the Pope, who for spite of your Christian religion, although he speak fair and seem as your friend by outward dealings, but inwardly secretly seeketh daily to study and procure by all ways he can not only to overthrow your Empire and the Gospel, but also the Queen of England and all other evangelical princes and countries: as is not unknown to your Graces and other imperial princes, how he taketh upon him by authority of his crafty general councils to pull down rightful emperors, kings, princes and states, and to set up and make such as pleaseth him. As how often since England received the Gospel hath the Popes given that kingdom to Emperor Charles and the French King. And now of late, since the reign of this good Queen who hath restored the Gospel, hath he not given the kingdom of England to King Philip and the French King, or to any other that would invade it. Thus he never ceaseth but with his cardinals, bishops and other his shavelings to overthrow the Gospel, daily studying and procuring war and discord between prince and prince.

Art. 62

What thinks your Graces, was meant when the Pope with his

Council of Cardinals and Bishops would have made King Philip an emperor, and for lack of a better place the Emperor of the Indians? Read Carion's *Chronicle* and other ancient writers, wherein you shall see what trouble was in Germany when the Pope took upon him authority to make emperors, or that by other means there was two emperors living at one time in Christendom. And how oftentimes the Pope and his Romans (since the election of the Emperor hath been in the hands of the German princes, which hath been from the year of our Lord 1003 that Otto the third Emperor of that name ordained it) have sought to bring the same election to Rome again, to him and his Romans, which hath been the occasion and death of so many German princes and people that it is lamentable to read. Maurice, Duke of Saxony and brother to Duke Augustus now Elector, fully declareth [this], as appeareth in the beginning of the four-and-twentieth book of Sleidan's, in his orations made to the princes of Germany against Emperor Charles, both for breach of promise in wrongful detaining in prison of the Landgrave and the Duke of Saxony, and for other violences used to the German princes, their people, towns and country. It maketh me to remember the witty saying and message that great Alexander of Macedon sent to Darius the Emperor of Persia and Media, which was, that it was not possible that two suns should shine at one time in the heavens with equality: meaning thereby, no more it was possible for two such great emperors as they were could reign together in Asia with quietness. The Pope thought, considering the great power and riches that King Philip hath by his dominions in Italy, Spain and other places, having once the name of an Emperor, [he] would beard face and be checkmate with the Emperor of Germany, and shortly by his help and with the help of his Cardinals, Bishops and other spiritual persons or people [he would] make him Emperor of Rome, and Germany also; and by that way and means he thinketh his devilish and popish kingdom might flourish again. But I am of Alexander's opinion, if thereby two Christian emperors living together in Christendom at one time will not only make much war, trouble and disquietness, but [be] also the next way and mean to bring in the Turk to drive us out of the rest of Christendom.

These be the right fruits and always spring from the Pope and his shavelings.

Art. 63

Your Graces will ask me, how dare the Pope be so bold to enterprise such things, because he is in such a league with King Philip, and King Philip with him, as almost cannot be broken off, of neither of their parts, for two considerations. The first is: King Philip in my opinion, by the advice of his Council rather observeth the great league and friendship with the Pope to have him his friend, for the more sure and quiet keeping under his obeisance the kingdom of Naples and Sicily, the dukedom of Milan and other his dominions in those parts of Italy, than for any love he beareth unto the Pope or his religion, or any malice he beareth the Gospel. For of nature, King Philip is a gentle and merciful prince, inclined to all peace and quietness. The second cause is: the Pope observeth this league and seeketh to please King Philip; [this] is for no love he beareth unto him but by reason he is the mightiest prince in Europe, and with his great treasures and dominions is best able to defend and keep him, and is the only defender and keeper of him in his abused authority and false religion. So that, considering how the Gospel is preached and known all Christendom through, and his popish and foolish traditions known to be wicked, abominable and to be abhorred, he will not break with King Philip. For if they two break, they be both in great danger, King Philip to lose his dominions in Italy, and the Pope to lose all his dominions, honour, power and reputation for ever. Which were the happiest thing that came to Christendom this thousand years.

Art. 64

Your Graces will ask me, what hurt doth the great league and friendship between King Philip and the Pope? It maketh not only all your bishops and other your spiritual people in Germany, but all other spiritual people and popish bishops in other regions (to the great hurt, trouble and disquietness of the Empire and them) who, knowing what the great power and riches the Pope and the King be of, maketh them to be so stout and, knowing how craftily their father the Pope can work, hope for such a day and time to come, that they may set up all Christendom through their popish and bloody kingdom again, and pause not for you and other their temporal princes, disclosing your counsels to those that they think may hinder you, and your godly proceedings in seeking out the Gospel, and further them in their devilish doctrine and treasons both against God, you and their country. And whether these things be a sufferable, honourable, profitable assurance and quietness to the imperial state and subjects, and other countries and kingdoms, I leave to your Graces and other princes of the Empire to consider. What mischiefs hath been in times past, and is now at this present time and will be in time to come, if the Pope may reign in his authority, and his shavelings, being sworn to his decrees which be both against God and his holy Gospel and all other godly proceedings and laws that good Christian princes make, may be suffered to sit in your Councils and be secret amongst you and other Christian princes, and be privy to all your doings, maketh me to think of and remember that wise, politic and mighty prince Emperor Charles the Fifth.

The Pope, knowing in what great authority and favour Granvelle the Bishop of Arras was with the said emperor, to make the said bishop his friend and to further all his popish and bloody doings, and the better to win him, sent Granvelle being the said Bishop of Arras a cardinal['s] hat, and would make him a cardinal. Wherefore the bishop, as all other be ambitious, was glad to come to the honour of a cardinal and thereby to be a king's fellow, and afterwards hoping to be the Pope and then to be above the Emperor, came to the Emperor his master full hypocritically and declared to His Majesty how his holy father the Pope of his goodness had sent him a cardinal's hat, and would forsooth if it please His Majesty make him a cardinal; most humbly beseeching his highness, in consideration of his good and faithful service done and to be done, both to His Majesty and to his son and countries (as you shall hereafter perceive his good service he hath done, and how well he deserved to be a cardinal, and what fruits came by them being cardinals as is said), he desired the Emperor to be his gracious prince and give him leave to receive that holy order and dignity of cardinalship. The Emperor which to his cost and trouble, being well acquainted with the policies of the Pope, what he meaneth and for what intent he maketh any man a cardinal, and wittily considering what would follow if he suffered him to be a cardinal, answered thus: he was glad to hear of anything that might be to his preferment, and was well contented that he should receive that hat and dignity of cardinalship, conditionally that was, that immediately after he was made cardinal, and taken the oath appertaining to a cardinal, [he was] straightway to pack him out of his court and council, and get him to Rome to his master and holy father the Pope; for, said he, thou canst not be a cardinal but thou must take an oath to be secret, true, obedient and faithful to the Pope and all his doings, and thou art sworn to be true, faithful, secret and obedient to me and all my doings. And thou only, knowest the secrets and bottom of my heart. Let me see then how thou canst observe both these oaths and deal justly and honestly: but either thou must serve God or Mammon. This bishop thus being truly touched by this wise and expert Emperor, whose witty answers in this case I wish all other princes to consider and follow. Thus this crafty bishop dissembled the matter at that time, and was content to lose his cardinal's hat. But he hath gotten it now; and what happened after he had gotten it, I pray you? He was no more bishop of Arras and subject, but a cardinal and King Philip's fellow. Was there any quietness amongst the princes and council of King Philip's Netherlands so long as he was amongst them? No, truly, but great trouble and variance. And against the will of most part of the princes and councillors of King Philip's Netherlands, he to please his master and father the Pope, for spite the Pope had to England for religion's sake, and by help and counsel of other French and Spanish cardinals his fellows and sworn servants to Rome, to make war betwixt England and King Philip, hath sought quarrels, controversies and questions, whereout is grown this variance and in manner breach of old friendship between England and the House of Burgundy which hath continued many years.

Whereupon the English merchants be departed from the

Netherlands. Here is the fruit that cometh by shavelings that be in authority and of princes' council, who to maintain and please their holy father the Pope; which Pope, in my opinion, would not much pause if all Christendom were Turkish, rather than he would lose his usurped authority and power.

Art. 65

But the old saying is, that it is an evil wind that bloweth no man to profit. This variance betwixt England and the House of Burgundy is happily happened for Germany, as I have declared, if the imperial princes will justly consider the same. Wherefore I cannot forget, but under your correction to put your Graces in remembrance of the example of the wise man who, being sick a little before his death, commanded all his sons into his presence, and had prepared a bundle of weak sticks bound fast together. Which bundle of sticks the father first delivered to the eldest son and bade him break it, which he proved to break but was not able; and so all the rest of his sons proved, one after another, and no one of himself was able to break this bundle. Then the father did cause the bands of this bundle to be broken, and delivered to every one of his sons a stick, and bade them prove if they could break them. Which before his face every one brake his stick easily, by reason every stick of itself being weak was not so strong as the bundle being bound together. Even so, most gracious princes of the Empire, it standeth with you and will stand with you so long as this power and treasure is at King Philip's commandment, he may use and practise the counsel that Granvelle the father of the Bishop of Arras, lying sick sent his last commendations or words that he spake to Emperor Charles, which was that if ever he will conquer Germany, either with money or otherwise, be sure to set the German princes at variance one with another; and then, having the Pope, your cardinal and bishops to friends, he will with his treasure corrupt some of your neighbours; or else, by such aid as he may have of your bishops and spirituality, be able with his treasure to make open war as his father did.

Thus this faggot will never be bound but either by this treasure or open war be divided. Thus this treasure being over in Germany at the commandment of the imperial princes (as the only quiet and plain way is declared how to get the same), then is no man able to undo or loose this faggot or unity that would be amongst you, by which unity the Pope will fear you, because King Philip his defender could no longer maintain him. For his treasures and milch cow being once gone from him, he shall have enough to defend his own dominions; which when all your spiritual and popish people shall perceive that you imperial princes be so strong and their two pillars to fail, in whom they have so long trusted, then they will fear, serve and obey you and your commandments; and though not in their hearts and consciences yet for fear of your authority and power, set out and suffer the Gospel to be generally preached. Whereby God shall be known, praised and feared, and his whole Gospel and commandments taught and preached, to the comfort of all Christian nations; your obstinate and popish people, that your shavelings have so long kept in disobedience and darkness, shall be taught to learn their obedience and duties both to God and you, their princes and rulers. Whereby great quietness, wealth and strength would ensue to all Germany and other Christian nations, to the fear of that fierce, mighty and cruel Turk when he shall hear of this wealth and traffic to be in your empire and at your commandment; and his secret and privy captain and soldier the Pope, who is the disturber of all Christian princes, to be reformed; unity and concord of religion to be in Germany, which country is only the heart, head and strength of all Christendom. What will then ensue thereof? God's mercy, peace, love and quietness will be amongst you, your people and subjects, whereout will grow great abundance of riches and wealth, and thus with quietness bring your country and the Empire of Germany to her former state; for which your Graces and other princes of the Empire now living shall have and receive immortal fame, like unto your most worthy progenitors.

Art. 66

[Earl of East Friesland *loq.*] You have satisfied me in all these things concerning the commodities of England; and both what profit cometh by buying and selling of the English merchants, and what benefits that country hath by them, where they settle themselves and their traffic. But yet, there is another thing which you have touched divers times in your talk, but make no further declarations or mention of it. [W.G. *loq.*] What is that? [Earl *loq.*] You have talked much of the amity of the English prince, and what profit and aid the House of Burgundy hath had thereby. Is England, then, of such force and power that the amity and friendship thereof is so necessary to the imperial State?

Art. 67

Yes, truly, as your Grace shall hear. First, I have declared to you what profit and benefit cometh to any town or country by the commodities of England, and where English merchants traffic, which I trust is so evidently proved, as your Grace doth confess there needs no further declaration thereof to be made. Now, under your Grace's correction, I will show my opinion as concerning the prince of England, not as one that taketh upon him to meddle with imperial affairs, or to appoint things of myself that appertain to your Grace and other our gracious lords the Electors, but as in this rude collection I have made my humble supplication to your Grace, not only to consider the present and dangerous state of the Empire, but also the loss of towns and countries from the same, as is declared, being thus consumed or as I may term it, stolen or pulled away, and by means of this traffic may be restored wholly to our Empire again: even so, to your Grace's request according to my bounden duty as a lover of my country and careful for the profit and commonwealth of the same, to show my opinion what I know, and have heard and read of the princes of England and, according to the talent or knowledge that God hath given me, committing the judgment therof to their Graces and your most godly and excellent wisdom to consider of the same, and what and how they and you shall think and determine of, the same I [am] as an obedient subject both to obey and keep.

But now, to come to speak of the nature and manner of the English prince and people, your Grace shall understand they be descended by blood and nature from our Dutch nation; as divers old Latin writers and English chronicles themselves do affirm that about the year of our Lord 500 or thereupon a Saxon duke named Ingest, with his people [whom] he brought out of Saxony, Friesland and Westphalia, came into the kingdom of England, being then named Great Britain; and in continuance of time, after many sharp battles [he] drove the people then inhabiting that country being named Britons into certain mountains lying in the furthest part of the north-west part of that kingdom, being now called Wales, where they remain to this day, still speaking the British language but yet subjects to the princes and people of England. So that then the said prince Ingest after his conquest changed the name of that country from Britain and called it Ingest's land after his own name, and now by alteration of time it is called England. Which people, as I have said, be descended from us, and sundry times since that conquest our emperors and princes of Germany have married the daughters of the kings of England. Their language in most words is like unto ours, agreeing with us in religion, of nature, manners, conditions and usage in most things agreeable with us; and thereof we have had good experience since their coming to traffic in your Graces' city of Emden. And whensoever they and we do meet in foreign countries, as in France or Italy, we be inclined to keep company and friendship together than either with Spanish, French or Italians. And how faithful those princes and nobility of England have ever been in observing all their leagues and promises they have made with foreign princes, the world knoweth, and in this book is and shall be declared. By nature, their people be not so much inclined to such crafts and deceits and troubles as some other nations be, with whom our imperial princes and the Dutch people have great traffic.

But now, to come to speak of this English prince who governeth at this present. She is a Lady of whom I must and will talk with all honour and reverence, not only in consideration of Her Majesty's sundry and most excellent virtues wherewith God hath endowed her, and specially for her zealous love to religion and the Gospel of Christ, but also for her great honour and fame [which] the princes of that noble kingdom have always deserved, wherein this most noble and godly queen is nothing inferior but rather exalteth [above] all other her noble progenitors, and in my opinion all other princes now living, as one whom God hath most principally blessed and marvellously defended from a great number of dangers and conspiracies both of domestical and foreign enemies. In wisdom she is a second Solomon, as by her noble, wise, quiet, blessed and merciful government doth appear, which the Lord long continue; whose noble progenitors and she for this six or seven hundred years have always been friends and in amity with the whole Empire and the princes of the same.

Art. 68

Therefore to go to my matter: your Graces know the duties of subjects to their sovereigns and princes, so that without the good will, favour and licence of the Queen of England the merchants, her subjects, will not enter to traffic in any place without her Majesty's pleasure first known and her good will had to the same, notwithstanding by the only ancient order and law of their country the merchants be free to travel into all places and countries of the world where it pleaseth them, being in amity with their prince. And now, at this breach or difference betwixt England and the Netherlands, as I am credibly informed and do know, the English merchants, having their liberty by consent of the queen to go with their commodities to any place of Europe where they thought most meetest for them to utter the same, except King Philip's Netherlands; and although divers towns and countries to have them with their commodities did not only offer great, ample and large privileges and freedoms, but also both to give and lend them great sums of money, yet the said English merchants, in respect of the old friendship and traffic that of long time hath been and yet is used betwixt the merchants of Germany and them as well in the marts at Bruges 120 years past as also sithence that time both at Middelburg and now at Antwerp to this day (which old friendship of the Empire and the imperial countries, towns and merchants they more esteemed without money than the new-proffered friends and friendship with money), did choose to come to the city of Emden being an imperial city, with their ships, goods and persons. Giving the

Queen's Majesty their soveriegn lady to understand upon what considerations they chose that place without money rather than other places with money: wherewith Her Majesty was content and very well pleased with their doings, and commended them that they had such respect [as] to traffic with their old friends, and specially being subjects and under the government of the whole Empire; and also in the town and country of such a prince as of old time their good wills by deeds have been found and proved ready both to please Her Majesty's father and brother; and after in the late time of persecution, such English people as fled for love of the Gospel, which be now her faithful subjects; which ancient amity of those princes, with the rest of the Princes Electors and other imperial princes, towns and countries Her Majesty more esteemed than any other [of] her Highness's allies and friends.

Thus your Graces may see both the good will and love of the English prince towards her subjects the merchants, and also how obedient those subjects be toward their prince that like as they will do nothing to displease her, so is she most ready and willing at all times to do anything that pleaseth them. So that you may see the prince is the only head, and her good will must first be gotten and then the merchants will follow; but as your Graces may see, here neither lacks the getting of the good will of the prince nor subjects, but [it] cometh as a thing unlooked for. And truly, it may be well thought to be appointed and ordained of God for some good and blessed purpose that they thus freely and of their own good will without mistrust, only upon your word and promise of honour, without asking such bonds or sureties as they had of the progenitors of the House of Burgundy, do come into your country and put themselves into your hands with such a great sum of treasure being the most noblest and profitablest commodities in the world. Whose happy and friendly coming, I pray God, your Graces and other gracious princes and governors may so consider as I have declared in the preface of this Book.

Art. 69

But now, to come to declare the strength and power of England and the English princes, and to see how commodiously England lieth for the aid and help of Germany, and what England is able to do for Germany in time of need, and how faithfully and honourably the English princes, although it hath been to their inestimable and incredible charges, have always observed and kept their leagues and amities with the House of Burgundy and all other princes, I will show what I have both read and know to be the most true.

Art. 70

After the Earldom of Flanders was knit unto the House of Burgundy by marriage, as is declared in the first article of this Book, the Burgundians thought no way or means might be so great assurance to them as to ally themselves with the King of England with some bonds or league. Which in time they brought to pass; and obtained of the King of England, yea, and as it is said, the King of England the rather granted to this league and amity for three considerations.

(1) The first was that the Kings of England since the time of Edward, the third king of that name, who by right of his mother Isabel daughter to King Philip of France, named Philip the Fair, to which Isabel the right inheritance and crown of France belonged after the death[s] of Lewis, Philip and Charles her brethren, sons to King Philip the Fair aforesaid, who died all without heirs male, which was about the year of our Lord 1327, the Kings of England, I say, quartered the arms of England and France. Which title hath caused much mortal war and bloodshed.

(2) The second cause was considering Calais, which the said Edward III had gotten from the French nation, stood betwixt France and Flanders; and the friendship of Flanders might be the more quiet keeping thereof in the English possession.

(3) And the third cause was that Flanders, Brabant, Zealand and Holland stood so commodiously and near unto England, and that the English merchants with the commodities of England were already settled in that country, as appeareth in the second Article of this Book.

The English princes in consideration of and for the more safeguard, quietness and commodity of these three matters were rather moved to this league, which hath continued from the time of the said King Edward III till now; but specially observed from the time of the fifth King Henry, King of England, and Duke [Philip?] of Burgundy, which King and Duke reigned about the year of our Lord 1420. Which league to this day was never broken; but at the death or change of any prince of either part the same league and intercourse hath been new confirmed and sometimes augmented, but specially augmented by Duke Philip, son to Maximilian Emperor, and father to Emperor Charles and grandfather to King Philip that now is. For the maintenance of which league and amity, it is openly known to all nations and countries how from the time after that Calais was gotten from the French nation by the third Edward King of England, which is about 218 years past, what great armies both by sea and land the kings of England have sent to invade France in the aid and for the quarrel of the House of Burgundy divers writers make mention; but specially since the beginning of the reign of Henry the fifth king of that name aforesaid, being in the year of our Lord 1412, in whose court Philip the Duke of Burgundy and father to Charles named Charles the Hardy (which Charles was slain before Nancy) was brought up in manner of a child. But to make some proofs of that I have spoken of, that they may appear to be credible, I will begin and show things that have been done in memory of men yet living. But before I enter to make my proofs, I must let your Graces to understand by the way, as I have declared, how England and the House of Burgundy were joined in league and friendship even so were France and Scotland: [so] that whensoever England had war with France, they were sure that Scotland would have war with England, so that England hath been forced always to make double war and prepare two armies, sometimes three, as shall appear.

Art. 71

Now, to go to my proofs. In the year of our Lord 1442,[15] which is 122 years past, Henry VII, King of England of that name and grandfather to this godly Queen that now is, in the aid and help of Maximilian, Duke of Austria and son to Frederick the Emperor, which Maximilian had married Mary

[15] *Recte* 1492.

the daughter and heir of Charles named Charles the Great or Hardy, Duke of Burgundy and Brabant, Earl of Flanders, Zealand, Holland &c., that was slain before Nancy aforesaid, against which Maximilian the most part of the towns of Flanders rebelled; when Dixmude in Flanders was besieged by the Flemings and Frenchmen at the procurement of the Flemings who rebelled against Maximilian aforesaid their rightful prince did not, say I, the said prince, King of England, at his own charges send an army into Flanders under the guiding of the Lord Daubeney and Lord Morley, and raised the siege and took all their ordnance and provision, and slew 8,000 Frenchmen and Flemings, and set the town at liberty?

Art. 72

In the year of our Lord 1493, did not the said King Henry send an army to Newport, a town in Flanders standing near unto the seas, which town at the request of the rebellious Flemings the Lord Querdes of France had besieged with 20,000 Frenchmen and Flemings and gotten and possessed one of the strongest towers or bulwarks of that town, whereby it stood in great danger. But at the coming of the English army, the Lord Querdes fled, with the loss of many of his men and much of his provision. And thus was that town delivered from their enemies.

Art. 73

In the year of our Lord God 1493, the said King Henry sent an army by seas to aid the said Maximilian against the Lord Ravenstein who had taken the haven and castle of Sluys, being the only port to the seas of that old famous town of Bruges. Which castle the Lord Poynings, general for the King of England, took from the said Lord Ravenstein by force and delivered the same to one Duke Albert of Upper Saxony, a captain and great friend to the said Emperor Maximilian. Which castle of Sluys and the town of Newport if the King of England had not defended and recovered the French King had recovered and overrun all the Earldom of Flanders and joined it to his Kingdom of France.

Art. 74

In the year of our Lord 1494, did not the said King of England at the request of Maximilian, for such shameful dishonour as the ninth Charles King of France of that name did unto the said Maximilian, not only in returning the Lady Margaret his daughter home to him again, to whom the said French King was by promise assured, and by such order as princes use by deputies married to her, but also violently and craftily getting from the said Maximilian the Lady and the only daughter and heir of the Duke of Brittany, to whom he was married; did not the said King Henry of England, I say, at the request of Emperor Maximilian to his great cost and charges, in his own royal person come over the seas with a great army, where Emperor Maximilian promised to meet him with another great army out of Flanders, to make war upon the French King? Also, for to revenge the great dishonour unto the said Emperor Maximilian, which Emperor at that time lacking both money and men came not to the King of England according to his promise, yet nevertheless the King of England proceeded in this war, and besieged Boulogne in France and wasted and burnt all the country thereabouts, getting great spoils; so [that] at the length the French King sued to him for peace, which upon certain conditions and payments of great sums of money were granted, to the great honour of the King of England. Which war being ended, the King of England returned home again and never heard of nor saw the Emperor Maximilian of all that time.

Art. 75

About the year of our Lord 1511, at the request of Emperor Maximilian, whose son and heir Philip had married Joan the daughter and heir of Ferdinand King of Spain, did not King Henry the eighth of that name, son to King Henry VII aforesaid and father to this queen, send out of England an army of 16,000 men by ship into Spain, in aid of King Ferdinand against the French King, who sought to invade part of Spain?

Art. 76

About the year of our Lord 1513 at the request of the said

Emperor Maximilian, in the defence of Charles the young prince or infant of Spain being but a child, which Charles was after emperor, whose countries the French king sought to spoil, invade and get from him, did not the said king Henry VIII in his own person with an army royal, come into France and laid siege to the strong city of Thérouanne? To rescue whereof came the power of France. Which siege the king both kept, and also overthrew and discomfited the French army in plein battle, and took prisoners the Duke [of] Longueville, the Marquess of Rothelin, the Lord of Clermont and the number of 240 lords, knights and gentlemen of name; and many common soldiers [were] slain in battle to the number of eight or ten thousand. To which battle Maximilian the Emperor came in person with certain noblemen of the Netherlands to the number of forty or fifty; which Maximilian and they all were under the King of England's standard and in his wages, and wore the red cross of St. George the English cognisance. So after this overthrow the city of Thérouanne was rendered to the King of England. And from thence the King went to the strong city named Tournai which was named to be a maiden city, never gotten by any prince. Which city he gat also, and then returned to England back again with triumph and glory. And now to come to Scotland: as I have said, at the time that the King of England was in France and lay before Thérouanne the King of Scotland who married the Lady Margaret, sister to the said King Henry of England, not past seven or eight years before, at which marriage he was sworn, and received, as they term it, the Holy Sacrament, to keep perpetual peace and amity with England; which his oath and promises (not regarding his duty to God's word, nor his honour to the world) he utterly refused, broke and with a sudden army unlooked for made sharp war upon the English lords. Against whom, the Duke of Norfolk and his son the Earl of Surrey, being then High Admiral of England, went with an army of Englishmen into Scotland, and in plein battle within Scotland in a place called Bramston overthrew and put to flight the whole power of Scotland being in number, as the Scottish stories make mention, 50,000 fighting men, and took all their artillery, provision and tents. In which battle the King of Scotland himself was slain with many of his nobility and gentlemen, and of common soldiers 13,000, and taken prisoners the number of 12 Earls, 20 lords, forty or fifty knights, besides gentlemen.

Art. 77

About the year of our Lord 1514, did not the said King Henry VIII send a band of soldiers into Gelderland under the guiding of the Lord Clinton at the request of the Lady Margaret, at that time being Regent of the Netherlands, to aid the Burgundians against the Duke of Gelder?

Art. 78

In the year of our Lord 1530, a perpetual peace being sworn at Paris in France betwixt Emperor Charles, the French King and the King of England, during their three lives; and which of them three did first violate or break that peace, the other two to set upon him with open wars as his enemies. Which league was first broken of the French King's part, for quarrel betwixt him and the Emperor Charles, [when] the King of England for his promise['s] sake, to aid the Emperor sent Charles the Duke of Suffolk into France with an army by land, and also a great army of ships by sea.

Art. 79

At which time as is aforesaid, the Duke of Albany in Scotland began to spoil the English Borders in the aid of France; against whom the King of England sent the Earl of Surrey. Who discomfited the said Duke of Albany and forced him to flee, to the great loss and dishonour of the Scots, whose country the Earl of Surrey aforesaid burnt, destroyed and returned back again with great praise and booties.

Art. 80

In the year of our Lord God 1543, did not the said King Henry VIII, in the aid of the Emperor Charles when he went to Landrecies, send a band of six or eight thousand men under the guiding of Sir John Wallop, knight, and other English gentlemen?

Art. 81

In the year of our Lord God 1545, did not King Henry VIII in his own person with two armies come over the seas in aid of Emperor Charles? At which time he got Boulogne. And how unfriendly the Emperor Charles made peace with the French King unknown to the King of England and in breaking of other faithful promises (as in the sixth book of Sleidan's *Chronicle* appeareth)! Which thing being done but as yesterday and yet so fresh in memory of men yet living, I need not to write further thereof.

Art. 82

But as in my first declaration of Scotland, at this beginning of war with France the Scots were busy and made robberies and spoils in England. Against whom, the King of England sent before he went to Boulogne the Earl of Hertford and the Lord Lisle, Admiral of England, which Lord Lisle was after Duke of Northumberland, into Scotland with an army by seas. At which time they burnt the rich town of Leith and Edinburgh, being the chief city of that kingdom, wasted and spoiled their country, burnt many villages, rased piles and castles, and overthrew many Scots and destroyed all their country thereabouts. These wars have the Kings of England taken in hand for the House of Burgundy; besides sundry great sums of money lent both unto Emperor Maximilian and Emperor Charles by King Henry VIII in time of their need, as may appear in the sixth book of Sleidan.

Art. 83

In the year of our Lord 1557 or therupon, did not Queen Mary, Queen of England, for to aid King Philip her husband (contrary to his bonds and promises before he married her) make war with France, and send an army under the guiding of the Earls of Pembroke, Bedford and Rutland with divers other nobles and gentlemen, to help King Philip to get St. Quentin; and also sent another great army by seas under the guiding of the Lord Clinton, High Admiral of England, and divers other noblemen, which landed in France in a county named Brittany and burnt and spoiled much of the same. By which wars with

France, England lost Calais, which the princes of England had kept in spite of all France 200 and odd years before that time; which wars after the death of Queen Mary this godly Queen, Queen Elizabeth that now reigneth, most honourably, godly and prudently ended. And what other privy and secret help the said Queen Mary gave unto King Philip her husband, that no man knew on. But it is thought to be many thousands of pounds; and by the opinion of wise men that be of experience and knowledge since that Maximilian, Emperor, grandfather to Charles that married the lady Mary daughter to Charles the Duke of Burgundy named Charles the Hardy aforesaid, whereby Maximilian was Duke of Burgundy, in defending of the Netherlands as is declared, it hath cost England above £6,000,000, and as some men will say, a great deal more.

Art. 84

How saith your Graces? Have not here been faithful and friendly princes and people, that thus truly have always holpen this House of Burgundy at their need? And yet, I reckon none of the wars made from the time of Edward III of England of that name to the beginning of the reign of Henry VII king of that name and grandfather to this Queen Elizabeth, which is about 144 years; but have only reckoned these wars that were done for this 70 years last past, being in memory of men yet living.

Art. 85

Your Graces will say, I have showed you many things done by the princes of England to charge the House of Burgundy withal; but have not the dukes and princes of the House of Burgundy never holpen the princes of England to war against Scotland and France? No, truly: I never read, knew nor heard that at any time for the only help of the English princes that ever the House of Burgundy made war with France or Scotland, or that ever the English princes asked their aid but once.

Which was by that godly young King Edward VI King of that name, son to King Henry VIII and brother to the Queen that now is, being but eight or nine years old, having war both with Scotland and France at one time, besides for alteration of religion clean abolishing and putting away the rest of the popish dirges and devilish doctrine, all the papists of England had moved and stirred the most part of the common people, all England through, to rebel against that godly prince and King. Which rebels in all places were thought to be in number 100,000 persons at the least; which afterward, God be thanked, by his help and good policy was well appeased with little hurt. At which time, this godly young King by the advice of his Council sent his sundry solemn and grave ambassadors to Emperor Charles for his aid, declaring not only the state of his infancy but also his great, chargeable and dangerous wars, which by his father King Henry VIII was taken and begun for his quarrel, besides the rebellion of his subjects: the said ambassadors putting the Emperor in remembrance of the friendship and aid that the King's Majesty's grandfather Henry VII and his son King Henry VIII had showed and done to Emperor Maximilian his grandfather, and also what aid King Henry VIII his master King Edward's father had given to His Majesty in his infancy when he was but a child and prince in Spain, and sundry times since, not only in sending great armies into France and Spain in his quarrel; but afore he was chosen Emperor, the said King Henry VIII travailed and wrote to his friends the princes of Germany, praying them to prefer him to the imperial crown; but also in consideration [that] the present war that England had then both with France and Scotland, as is declared, was begun at the request and for the ancient amity and quarrel for the House of Burgundy.

All which things, it seemed, Emperor Charles had forgotten and would not remember, but [behaved] like as [when] he did forget the great friendship done to him by Duke Frederick, father to Duke John of Saxony (which Duke Frederick made him Emperor, as appeareth in the first and seventh book of Sleidan's *Chronicle*). But, as before said, the Emperor would not remember nor acknowledge any help, friendship or benefit done to him by the King of England, but gave the English ambassador uncourteous and sharp words for the King's religion with other unreasonable demands, and said, if the King of England would receive his *Interim*[16] and change his

[16] A compromise settlement imposed by the Emperor in 1548.

religion, then he would do many great things for him; or else, he would do nothing. Which, when the English ambassadors perceived and understood the Emperor's policies and meanings that he would give no aid to the King, they required His Majesty that he would do so much as take Boulogne into his hands, which not long before King Henry VIII of England had gotten from the French King (as in the seventy-ninth article), requiring His Majesty to be a defender thereof for a time, till the King of England had pacified his troubles at home and set his subjects in quietness; and for such charges [as] His Majesty should be put in keeping thereof, they should be justly and truly paid him. Which the Emperor refused and would not do unless the King would change his religion, which the King of England would not do. But he and his godly council, having the fear of God in their hearts, refused; and chose rather to lose earthly things than heavenly.

This good will and help had the King of England of the Emperor in time of his need. He would neither help himself, nor suffer any kind of munition or soldiers to go out of his dominions into England, no, not so much as to one of the English ambassadors, who had bought a harness for his own person at Brussels. He would not suffer it to pass. These unfriendly and rather cruel dealings caused the King of England about the year of our Lord 1549 to make peace with France and Scotland. Which peace betwixt England and France was no profit to the Emperor and to the House of Burgundy, for immediately after following, in the year of our Lord 1551 began the great wars betwixt the Emperor Charles and Henry, the French King that was killed at the tilt; which war the Burgundish felt when they lacked the English power by sea and by land, but specially by sea.

Art. 86

Thus your Graces may see, if the Kings of England had not continually holpen the House of Burgundy and the Netherlands they had been French before this day; or if the French Kings might have been sure to have had England to have been an indifferent friend and to have sitten still and looked on, that French Kings might, without the fear of England always, have bent their whole power both by sea and land against the House of Burgundy and Spain, Emperor Charles had neither gotten so much advantage of the French King as he hath done, neither had been able to have troubled German princes nor other princes, states and countries as he hath done, neither had gotten and possessed so many dominions in Italy and other places, nor his subjects obtained so much wealth, riches and knowledge both by sea and land as they now have gotten by policy, both of their own and of other strange nations; but by the aid only of the English princes and traffic of the English merchants, as in this book is expressed at large. Which aid, strength, traffic and riches our imperial state and princes may have if they will; considering all these inestimable charges which the Kings of England have been at and sustained in defending the House of Burgundy hath been for the three causes alleged in the second and sixty-ninth article of this book, but specially for two of the three causes.

Whereof the first was for the more quiet and sure keeping of Calais and the territories of the same under the English obeisance. The second cause was by reason that those countries as Brabant, Flanders, Zealand, Holland, stood so near and commodiously to England, and that if the English merchants had already stapled their commodities there and might travel thither easily and in manner without danger, which two causes only breed the amity between the House of Burgundy and England but now [are] wholly removed. For, as I have said in the eighty-second article of this book, the French King hath gotten Calais again, whereby it is thought to be utterly lost from the English nation and for the use and trade that English merchants were wont to have to Antwerp and in the Netherlands. By their own unfriendly dealing with the English princes and people, they be gone from them and be come to your Graces' town of Emden; and in my opinion they may be easily kept there still (seeing these two causes chiefly be removed, which hath continually caused the English princes to defend the Netherlands so far) if your Graces and other our good lords the princes Electors be willing to the same, namely to cherish and maintain the English merchants as is declared, whereby that mighty princess and profitable nation, as I have said, may be joined in amity with our imperial state, and your imperial state with their kingdom, which would bring us both great wealth and assurance in short time, as is declared, and be a helper and defender for our empire in time of need, and we the like defenders to their kingdom again, as your Graces may see they have been to the House of Burgundy both by sea and land.

Therefore it is wisdom to consider not only what power and strength King Philip is of, as is declared in the thirty-seventh article, but also to consider how the power and strength of Germany is decayed both in countries, towns, riches and people; and also what was meant when the Pope would have made King Philip an emperor, and seeks this great friendship and league with Maximilian our new King of the Romans. It is not to be liked, if you will justly consider the same, and mark the end, what will come thereof, and what is meant thereby. I have partly touched the danger in the thirty-first article of this book; and also, if your Graces may please to read the first book of Sleidan's *Chronicle*, there you shall plainly see and find in the orations that were made by the princes Electors for the election of Emperor Charles, how that true German and imperial bishop the Bishop [of] Trier the Elector, whose grave and politic wisdom foreseeing all these dangers that be now happened to Germany, like a true man and a lover of the liberty of his country and commonwealth, persuaded [the other Electors] to have a mere German prince made Emperor. Which when he could not obtain, by reason the good Duke Frederick of Saxony, being chosen, refused to be Emperor and gave his election to Emperor Charles, did not that good Bishop with lamentable words truly, as it were, complain and prophecy what would follow by the election of Emperor Charles, and what these Houses of Spain and Austria would come to.

Wherefore once again I say to your Graces out of a zealous heart and careful for Germany, I cannot but put your Graces and our gracious lords the Electors and other German princes in remembrance, to consider how France, Spain and Italy be changed from the state they were of, and become more puissant than they were in times past; and our imperial state become much weaker than in times past. Wherefore I pray unto

God you may foresee these great dangers in time, and make you strong with some outward friends as I have declared; which might be easily, if the prince and nation of England were once knit to you, and you to them, in league, friendship and traffic. Who then durst stir or attempt war against either of you, or trouble you, considering the great invincible power you both together be of: that is, the power of your German princes is invincible by land, and the Queen of England and that nation be invincible by seas and be likewise of great power by land, as appeareth by the great armies sent into France or Scotland, which were never foiled but always turned again with victory and honour. And the German princes and England being joined together, what merchant people in this hither part of Europe can travel or traffic from one region to another by seas or by land but must come or go in danger of Germany or England? Or, if the Pope or his Italians should attempt or conspire against you, what traffic could Italy have by land but it must come through our country into the Netherlands, if the marts do continue there, where you may easily meet with them; and if they will come into the Netherlands by seas, then the Queen of England with her invincible ships meets with them. Or, if King Philip and his friends, who have compassed you about with dominions, as appeareth in the thirty-seventh article, would seek to trouble you as his father Emperor Charles did, what could he do, or they, or what traffic or help can come to his Netherlands from Italy, but it must pass through your country and be in your danger? And coming out of Spain or Italy by seas, how can they escape the ships of the Queen of England, and other nations, which in number swarm upon the seas like bees? Or, what power of soldiers or traffic could come to King Philip's Netherlands, considering your imperial princes with your seigniories and dominions, which as it were do compass his Netherlands round about by land? And then, England is upon his back by seas, [so] that unless he will turn all his traffic and substance through France, which is so far about that the great charges would not only eat out their gains; but also, they would be in doubt or fear to put or trust so much substance in the French country, considering they have been ancient old enemies, and in manner continual war betwixt France and them; and to bring men of war through France to help them, the Frenchmen might think King Philip would do by them as they did by Metz in Lorraine.

Thus, having the English nation joined in league with you, and you with them, whose faithful princes hath been so honourable and truly kept with the House of Burgundy, either of you both may always be sure to have a strong and mighty friend at your back in time of need; and either to help [the] other both by seas and land. For like as your imperial state is the strongest part of Europe by land, so is England the strongest by seas. Thus being joined together as aforesaid, and having the traffic within the imperial state, who is able to withstand you when they can travel or traffic no way, but of force must come in one of your dangers? And then force will cause all nations both to fear and please you, whereout will come and grow all those blessings of God, and many moe, to Germany and England and to the rest of the whole Christian state, as I have written in the sixty-fifth article of this book. Therefore, to conclude and make an end, as I have said in the preface and other places of my book, in my opinion there is no nation in Europe that may be so profitable and necessary for the strength and assurance of the imperial state and subjects as England is, nor no country, nation nor people in Europe so profitable and necessary for the strength and assurance of England as Germany is in all respects and considerations.

Your Graces may see by these sundry examples and proofs in this my rude book, which book I most humbly beseech you to take in good part, and consider all things herein written to the best, according to my true meaning and to the goodwill, duty and obedience that I do owe unto your Graces and the imperial state, being a true subject and a poor member of the same. Which state, together with your Graces, according to my bounden duty I do daily pray to God and wish may prosper happily with all the rest of you German princes through the might of his grace and holy spirit, that all things that you do and take in hand may be to his glory and the increase of the Gospel, to the rest, peace and quietness of all Christian princes and specially to the honour, profit and assurance of Germany. The German princes and people beseeching you and their Graces all specially to have in remembrance and not to forget these few lines or notes following:

1. First, to cherish and maintain English merchants, and all other merchants that be willing to come and traffic within the imperial state.

2. That our free liberty and ancient customs may be maintained, and free traffic generally to be had, all Germany or the imperial state through; and that no such commandment or proclamations hereafter take place within Germany or the imperial borders as King Philip sent this last year, set out as appeareth in the thirty-fifth article of this book.

3. That no new tolls, excises or customs be raised within the imperial state or [any] member of the same.

4. That the mouth of the Rhine may be free for all German and imperial subjects to pass into and out of the seas to all parts of the imperial state without let or trouble, for such considerations as appeareth from the thirtieth article of this book to the thirty-eighth article.

5. That the city of Groningen and the country thereabouts may be under the defence and commandment of the empire; that thereby the river of Ems, the only jewel of the Empire, may be in safety from such dangers as I have declared in the thirty-first article of this book.

6. That the Earldom of Lingen must be restored to them that of right ought to have it, and that the heir be bound never to sell the same or seek any defender but only of the temporal princes Electors.

7. And in my opinion, if it may stand with the imperial laws, it were good that no towns or countries, being members of the Empire, from henceforth should make any prince their defender, not being mere imperial; for avoiding such dangers [as are] written from the thirty-first to the thirty-seventh article of this book.

8. That the Fuggers and the rest of the German merchants may be commanded to keep their habitations, with their wives and families, in some imperial town and country; and not to inhabit in Antwerp as they do, but by their factors; for avoid-

ing such dangers as appeareth in the thirty-eighth article of this book.

Art. 87

A re-warning given to my gracious lords the Earls of East Friesland, the first day of September 1572.

Considering, my most gracious lords, since the making of this book which was in the year of our Lord 1564, being now eight years past, many things written in the same, whereof at that time I gave your Graces and other imperial princes warning, according to my sayings and admonitions are now proved true and do cause me, being careful of Germany my country, even foreseeing the rest of the dangers whereof I have written to be coming towards you, are again [coming?] to put you in remembrance how it behoveth you not slightly but diligently and substantially to consider and weigh the contents and meaning written in the same book. For of one part it directeth you the true plain way and means not only how to obtain and bring both to yourselves, your country and subjects, and to the country and subjects of other imperial princes your neighbours great wealth, assurance and quietness, but also to avoid the great dangers, treasons and mischiefs that hang over you, and [for] many years have been meant, practised and partly executed upon your Graces and them. For like as you have found and see my sayings to prove true, how towns and countries where English merchants traffic do flourish and wax rich, as by example what Hamburg your neighbour hath attained to in few years, so in like manner you see how countries and towns decay and wax poor in few years from whence the English merchants depart, as by example of Antwerp. Therefore, like as these proofs be sufficient causes to cause you to be moved and other princes to follow my counsel in obtaining such inestimable benefits sundry ways to you and your subjects as my book declareth, even so, other examples and warnings which I have given you of the dangers that you be wrapped in ought in like manner to cause you to study with all care and diligence to foresee them, and seek remedy betimes. For now of late, according to my forewarnings, you see King Philip hath not only gotten into his possession the town of Groningen and begins to build a castle there, the danger whereof I most earnestly gave you to understand eight years past; but also, according to my sayings, he is come here unto your Graces, and that he began and attempted to build a fort under your nose at Delfzijl upon the river of Ems. Which although, by reason of his other troubles he hath now in hand, he dissembles and forbeareth the finishing of for a time, your Graces may be assured [that] when he hath quietness, and time do serve for his purpose, he will settle such a garrison and strength of Spaniards there that he will not only have that river at such commandment that neither yourself, your subjects nor none other [of] your friends or allies shall pass with their ships into or out of the same, but by his licence.

But also, in the end you and your country shall hardly escape but be oppressed and both be brought under the obedience and slavery of the Spaniards' government: the example whereof both your Graces and all other princes your neighbours may daily and plainly see by the tyranny, oppressions, wrongs and slaveries that be used in the *stift* of Utrecht, Gelderland, in Groningland, and other towns and countries of the Empire which King Philip now possesseth and holdeth of the Empire by no manner of right or inheritance, but only upon certain promises and conditions. And yet without any regard or fear thereof, but contrary to his oath, faith and promise, not passing of any duty he oweth towards the Empire, he breaks their ancient liberties, customs and freedoms, making such new orders and laws as pleaseth him, raising new charges, exactions and payments that were never used, to the perilous example of others. Whereby all wise men do and may plainly see [how] he pretended by little and little to bring the slavery and tyranny used in Naples amongst them of that country: and after upon you if he obtain his purpose. And hereof I have given your Graces and other princes warning eight years past; and foreseeing these evils aforehand which be right upon you, [it] made me in manner to cry unto you to seek a remedy in time as from the thirtieth to the thirty-ninth article of my book is largely discoursed, prognosticating aforehand unto you not only these evils past but other, that be not yet, to come. Which doubtless will both shortly and suddenly fall upon you ere you be aware, unless with more care and diligence you seek to prevent them than hitherto you have done.

For let both Germany, and England and all other princes and countries and towns that profess the Gospel be assured that, according to my former writing and adminitions written, from the sixty-first to the sixty-sixth article of my book, that the Pope, his cardinals, bishops and his other shavelings cease not [to] invent and conspire all manner of ways and treasons they can devise to overthrow religion, and specially in Germany and England. Which things do now burst out and openly appear to all the world by these most horrible, cruel, unmerciful, unnatural and shameful murders committed of late in France by the French king, contrary to his oath, faith and promise, whereby all men may plainly perceive this great dissembling league made of late at the Council of Trent betwixt the Emperor, King Philip, the French king, the King of Portugal, the Pope, the Venetians and other princes and states of Italy, under the name and colour to withstand and invade the Turk, was nothing meant that way, but only pretended under the colour of war against the Turk to make themselves strong and in readiness suddenly to persecute the professors of the Gospel as the French king hath done, now taking for the defence of this his wicked and bloody deeds the old sayings of papists, there is no faith or promise to be kept with heretics.

Doubtless it is most like, our popish princes and bishops in Germany be secretly agreed with them. Which giveth great cause to all princes and states that profess the Gospel, and specially the princes of Germany and the Queen of England and the princes and states of Eastland, to join together and look to themselves in time, and take example of the doings and sayings of the wise men, of whom I have written in the sixty-fifth article of my book; which things if they will follow, that England and Germany be joined together in brotherly love, no doubt but God will bless and prosper them and their doings, and they shall be able to withstand all the power, crafts, malice, conspiracies and treasons of the Pope and all his adherents. Where otherwise, if they join not together in friendship as they do in religion, but divide themselves, not caring one for another, or if they do see their neighbour's house afire and take no regard to their own, in the end both Germany and England will be oppressed with these bloody tyrants.

And surely, as I have declared through all the discourse of my book, it stands your Graces most upon, and you must and ought to be the chiefest and only instruments and means that this league and amity may be made. In doing whereof, you ought not [to] spare any travail and diligence or friends to bring this good deed to pass. For as the country by the means of the river of Ems must be the only place and way whereby to join England and Germany together, even so must yourself, being as it were a middle or indifferent person, take pains and make labour to your friends and neighbours to join with you and help you therein. For when they shall understand by you of what great importance and how needful this league is to be made betwixt England and you for a general assurance and quietness of all Evangelical princes, if they have any regard at all to themselves, their country and prosperity, they will be as willing and ready to help as your Graces do desire. Which thing if you can attain and bring to pass, you shall not only thereby benefit yourselves and subjects the most, but you shall obtain immortal fame by doing so good a service both to your own country and divers others. Beseeching God to give his graces to you and other princes and to the Queen of England one with another, that his holy spirit may so work and move all their hearts to join brotherly together one with another, and to maintain and defend the profession of the Gospel, the liberty of your country, and to comfort and help poor afflicted members of Christ, for now comes the times of danger and troubles. Therefore despise not my counsel and warning.

Index

This index is intended to enable readers to locate mentions of particular persons or topics. It does not include references to names of frequent occurrence, such as Netherlands, East Friesland, Emden, Antwerp among places, nor Philip II, queen Elizabeth, the House of Burgundy and the Pope among persons, nor such general categories as artificers, merchants, princes.